WALKING

RIPON & LOWER WENSLEYDALE

HILLSIDE GUIDES - ACROSS THE NORTH AND BEYOND

The Uplands of Britain - full colour hardback books
- THE HIGH PEAKS OF ENGLAND & WALES
- YORKSHIRE DALES, MOORS & FELLS

Hillwalking - Lake District
- LAKELAND FELLS - SOUTH
- LAKELAND FELLS - NORTH
- LAKELAND FELLS - EAST
- LAKELAND FELLS - WEST

Long Distance Walks
- COAST TO COAST WALK
- DALES WAY
- CLEVELAND WAY
- WESTMORLAND WAY
- FURNESS WAY
- LADY ANNE'S WAY
- BRONTE WAY
- CALDERDALE WAY
- PENDLE WAY
- CUMBRIA WAY
- NIDDERDALE WAY
- TRANS-PENNINE WAY

Circular Walks - Yorkshire Dales
- WHARFEDALE
- MALHAMDALE
- SWALEDALE
- NIDDERDALE
- THREE PEAKS COUNTRY
- WENSLEYDALE
- HOWGILL FELLS
- HARROGATE & WHARFE VALLEY
- RIPON & LOWER WENSLEYDALE

Circular Walks - Peak District
- NORTHERN PEAK
- CENTRAL PEAK
- EASTERN PEAK
- SOUTHERN PEAK
- WESTERN PEAK

Circular Walks - Lancashire
- BOWLAND
- PENDLE & THE RIBBLE
- WEST PENNINE MOORS

Circular Walks - North West
- ARNSIDE & SILVERDALE

Circular Walks - North Pennines
- TEESDALE
- EDEN VALLEY
- ALSTON & ALLENDALE

Circular Walks - North York Moors
- WESTERN MOORS
- SOUTHERN MOORS

Circular Walks - South Pennines
- ILKLEY MOOR
- BRONTE COUNTRY
- CALDERDALE
- SOUTHERN PENNINES

---

*Send for a detailed current catalogue and price list
and also visit www.hillsidepublications.co.uk*

WALKING COUNTRY

RIPON & LOWER WENSLEYDALE

Paul Hannon

Hillside

HILLSIDE
PUBLICATIONS
9 Thorncliffe Road
Fell Lane
Keighley
West Yorkshire
BD22 6BY

First published 2007

© Paul Hannon 2007

ISBN 978-1-870141-82-6

Cover illustration: West Tanfield
Back cover: Coverham from under Braithwaite Moor;
Fountains Abbey; Grewelthorpe
Page One: The Devil's Arrows, Boroughbridge
Page Three: Old guidepost, Pott Valley
(Paul Hannon/Hillslides Picture Library)

The sketch maps in this book are based upon
1947 Ordnance Survey One-Inch maps

Printed in Great Britain by
Carnmor Print
95-97 London Road
Preston
Lancashire
PR1 4BA

CONTENTS

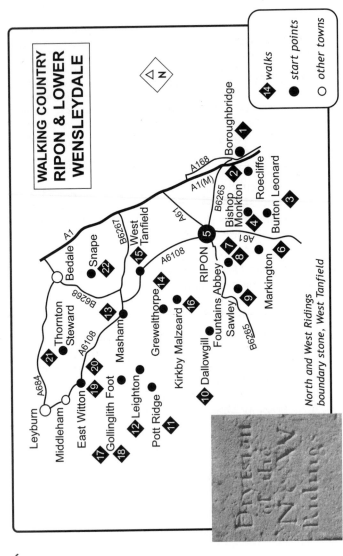

WALKING COUNTRY
RIPON & LOWER WENSLEYDALE

N △

Key:
- 14 walks
- ● start points
- ○ other towns

Boroughbridge

A168
A1(M)

Roecliffe

Bishop Monkton

Burton Leonard

A61
B6265

West Tanfield

A1

Bedale

Snape

B6267

RIPON

A6108

A61

Fountains Abbey

Sawley

Markington

B6265

Grewelthorpe

Kirkby Malzeard

Dallowgill

Masham

A6108

Thornton Steward

A684

Leyburn

Middleham

East Witton

Gollinglith Foot

Leighton

Pott Ridge

B6268

Walk numbers: 1, 2, 3, 4, 5, 6, 7, 8, 9, 10, 11, 12, 13, 14, 15, 16, 17, 18, 19, 20, 21, 22

North and West Ridings boundary stone, West Tanfield

6

INTRODUCTION

Those who think the attractions of Wensleydale end at the Yorkshire Dales National Park boundary will miss out on a multitude of delights. Unlike its neighbour the Swale, when the River Ure leaves the park near Middleham it still has a wealth of absorbing countryside to travel through, leading by way of Jervaulx Abbey, Masham and West Tanfield to the tiny cathedral city of Ripon, and on to the Great North Road at Boroughbridge. Allied to this, within its graceful curve the Ure embraces an upland scene where rolling heather moors are drained by the tributary rivers of the Burn, Laver and Skell.

This area, featuring delightful Colsterdale and Dallowgill, has its landscape value recognised by inclusion in the Nidderdale Area of Outstanding Natural Beauty - even though it all belongs to the Ure rather than the Nidd. Unjustly excluded when the national park was created, much of this countryside is unquestionably worthy of the highest designation. And within it stands one of the brightest jewels in the Yorkshire crown, none other than Fountains Abbey. As if its impressive ruins in a beautiful setting weren't enough, they are equalled by the adjacent water gardens and deer park of Studley Royal: simply stunning!

Ripon is very much the focal point for this area, being well sited for the A1 and offering all manner of attractions and accommodation. Its glory is its imposing cathedral, a major landmark for miles around. The Ure's banks also support a couple of charming old market towns: Boroughbridge oozes history with two battle sites, a Roman town and the remarkable Devil's Arrows, while the splendid little town of Masham is based around a massive square and is home to two celebrated breweries. Delightful villages abound too, including Sawley and Fearby, Bishop Monkton and Kirkby Malzeard, East Witton and Constable Burton. Most feature old cottages stood back from spacious greens, sometimes with duck-laden ponds at their heart, and usually with a welcoming pub to hand.

The area's wilder natural features are spread around the extensive Ilton, Braithwaite, Agra and Pott Moors, with a glimpse into Nidderdale at Thrope Edge. Here you will discover the hugely characterful gritstone outcrops of Combs Crags, Slipstone Crags and Gollinglith Crags, along with old moorland boundary stones and guideposts hidden in the heather.

The endearing ruins of Jervaulx Abbey concede little to Fountains in their romantic parkland setting by the Ure. You will encounter some splendid old houses at Newby Hall, Snape Castle and Markenfield Hall, along with further intriguing historic features at Well, Castle Steads and Lacon Cross.

The area is rich in remarkable curiosities such as the Druid's Temple at Ilton, the follies of Hackfall Woods at Grewelthorpe, and the Greygarth Monument. Equally diverse, lesser known highlights include Aldfield Spa, Sleningford Mill, Eavestone Lake and the Milby and Westwick Cuts that made the Ure navigable to Ripon, where a canal offers towpath delights. Add to this a forgotten wartime training area, a mosaic trail, the revitalised Wensleydale Railway, and the surrender to the all-embracing Ure of the beautiful rivers Swale, Cover, Burn and Skell.

Access to the countryside

The majority of walks in this guide are on public rights of way with no access restrictions, or long-established access areas and paths. A handful also take advantage of the 2004 implementation of 'Right to Roam'. This new freedom allows more logical routes to be created: such walks are noted in their introduction. Existing access areas and concession paths now largely fall within these vast swathes of Open Country, and on most days of the year you are free to walk responsibly over these wonderful landscapes. Of various restrictions that do pertain, the two most notable are that dogs are normally banned from grouse moors (other than on rights of way); and also that the areas can be closed to walkers for up to 28 days each year, subject to advance notice being given. Inevitably the most likely times will be from the 'Glorious Twelfth', the start of the grouse shooting season in August, though weekends should largely be unaffected. Further information can be obtained from the Countryside Agency (see page 95), and ideally from information centres. Finally, bear in mind that in springtime, avoiding tramping over open country, away from paths and tracks would greatly help to safeguard the most crucial period for vulnerable ground nesting birds.

Though bus services within the area are generally limited, availability, if any, is mentioned in the introduction to each walk. The nearest railway stations are at Harrogate and Northallerton, while the Wensleydale Railway also skirts the northern edge of the area.

Using the guide

The walks range from 5 to 9 miles, with the average distance being around 6$\frac{1}{2}$ miles. Each walk is self-contained, with essential information being followed by a concise route description and a simple map. Dovetailed in between are notes and illustrations of features along the way. Snippets of information have been placed in *italics* to ensure that the essential route description is easier to locate. The sketch maps serve to identify the location of the routes rather than the fine detail, and whilst the description should be sufficient to guide you around, the appropriate Ordnance Survey map is strongly recommended.

To gain the most from a walk, the detail of the 1:25,000 scale Explorer map is unsurpassed. It also gives the option to vary walks as desired, giving an improved picture of your surroundings and the availability of linking paths. Four maps cover this book's walks:

• *Explorer 298 - Nidderdale*
• *Explorer 299 - Ripon & Boroughbridge*
• *Explorer 302 - Northallerton & Thirsk*
• *Explorer OL30 - Yorkshire Dales North/Central*

Also extremely useful for planning is Landranger map 99 (Northallerton & Ripon) at the 1:50,000 scale, which conveniently covers the entire area.

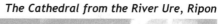

The Cathedral from the River Ure, Ripon

1

MYTON-ON-SWALE

START Boroughbridge   Grid ref. SE 396668

DISTANCE 7^{1}2 miles (12km)

ORDNANCE SURVEY MAPS
1:50,000
Landranger 99 - Northallerton & Ripon
1:25,000
Explorer 299 - Ripon & Boroughbridge

ACCESS Start from the town centre. Car park on Back Lane. Served by bus from Ripon, Harrogate and York. If mid-walk refreshment is desired start at Myton, putting Boroughbridge halfway round.

> Two battlefields feature in this dead-flat ramble visiting the confluence of the great Dales rivers of Ure and Swale

Boroughbridge is an ancient little town on the south bank of the River Ure, which now sports a marina, with boat trips. The town's centuries-old strategic setting on the Great North Road was eclipsed by construction of the A1 by-pass in 1963: the Crown Hotel is a survivor from coaching days, when it provided stabling for 100 horses. Of many attractive corners the cobbled Hall Square is delightful, with its war memorial, traditional cottages, and the Hall itself set back in its grounds. Also cobbled, the larger St James Square sports a resplendent fountain of 1875, enclosed by stone pillars supporting a red-brick canopy: the well beneath is over 250 feet deep, once the townsfolks' major water supply. Close by is the parish church of St James, dating from 1852.

Perhaps Boroughbridge is best known for the Devil's Arrows on the edge of town, three enormous gritstone monoliths aligned on a north-south line. Two of these menhirs stand in a field centre, the other plum on the roadside. *Averaging 20 feet in height, they are thought to be of religious significance and date from late Neolithic or early Bronze Age times. Also only half a mile distant at Aldborough is the site of the Roman town of Isurium, dating from around AD72, with a small museum in this lovely village.*

From Hall Square turn right on Fishergate to the Crown, then go right on Bridge Street to cross the bridge. *This great three-arched structure has a centuries-old history, but was widened in 1949. A wooden bridge stood here in 1322 when the Battle of Boroughbridge was fought between King Edward II's army under Sir Andrew Harcla and rebel forces led by the Earls of Lancaster and Hereford. The modern age inflicts itself on the scene with the incessant rumbling of traffic on the adjacent A1, now a motorway.*

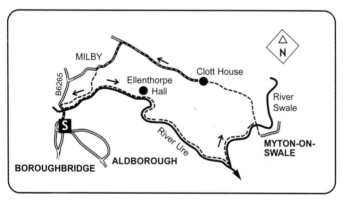

Immediately over the bridge turn right, and a splendid path heads downstream with the calm Ure. Before long a parallel path is seen to the left - this traces Milby Cut, to soon merge at Milby Lock. *This is one of six constructed in the late 18th century to make the Ure navigable as far as Ripon in order to facilitate river-borne trade.* Cross the footbridge and resume downstream over a stile. From here no instruction is necessary as this is effectively a riverbank walk all the way to Myton Bridge. A lush riverside sward leads past the red-brick frontage of Ellenthorpe Hall, with its walled garden and farm buildings. Unlike the map, the path clings tightly to the riverbank here.

Forge on past a scruffy corner before a sturdy grass embankment comes in. This makes an alternative to the riverbank, and leads unfailingly all the way to the confluence with the Swale. En route is the big double bend known as Hall Arm, while Aldborough is seen across the river. The approach of the Swale is foreseen when an embankment appears to the left. The bank cuts a little corner, but make your way to the very end, where a grassy nab makes a super spot to sit and contemplate. *For those of us who've spent many years cross-crossing the Dales, there's a certain mov-ing sensation here as two of its great rivers finally meet. Harder to discern is whether the water is actually moving!*

Your way is the only possible way, upstream with the narrower Swale. The river winds around to a kink where the tree-lined Myton Pasture Stell comes in, after which the embankment is deflected from the river by trees before meeting to reach Myton Bridge. *Not seen until you're virtually upon it, this fine iron arch was only restored in 2002: the original bridge of 1868 built by the Stapyltons of Myton Hall (as a toll bridge to replace a centuries-old ferry) had been declared unsafe in 1998. A mighty specimen to carry no more than a bridleway, it certainly makes for a quality last crossing of the Swale. The Battle of Myton took place here in 1319, when some 15,000 battle-hardened Scots made light work of around 10,000 English led by the Archbishop of York. Such was the numbers of ecclesiastics among the ill-fated English ranks that it became known as the White Battle.* Immediately across the bridge a rough road runs the few yards to the end of Myton's street. *There's not much going on here, just a red-brick former school of 1847 with a novel canopied bell still in place, and St Mary's church, restored in 1888. In its parkland just past the eastern end of the village is the impressive Myton Hall, the old seat of the Stapyltons.*

Retrace steps to the bridge, across which a grassy track takes over, becoming a pathway between hedgerows. *On your left is the battle site, hard to visualize today.* At the end take the left-hand of two gates and resume along a hedgeside to the substantial line of trees ahead. Swinging left with them, a grassy cart track takes over to run to the far corner. Here leave the continuing rougher track in favour of a bridle-gate just to the left, from where a fine grass track runs along the fieldsides to Clott House Farm.

Keep straight on the access road of Ellenthorpe Lane heading away. *Two of the three houses here bear coats of arms, the first most elaborate one of George V, dated 1927.* Almost at once you are joined by an access road from extensive Ellenthorpe Lodge over to the left. Remain on this road, hedgerowed and traffic-free all the way to a junction. Just after Ellenthorpe Hall Lodges there's an opportunity to divert through a hedge into a parallel fieldside for a couple of minutes. Reaching a junction with a through road, turn left for a less endearing few minutes into the hamlet of Milby.

On the bend is a nice green, with an attractive house to the right. Cross to a seat and cul-de-sac road heading away left. This leads past a few houses to terminate alongside Crown Farm. A lovely grassy cart track takes over, and within a couple of minutes you find yourself back on the riverbank beneath Milby Lock. *Just before this are the scant remains of the North Eastern Railway's Boroughbridge branch, from Knaresborough to the main line at Pilmoor Junction.* Return over the footbridge at the lock, and for a varied finish remain on the path shadowing the Milby Cut, soon becoming tightly enclosed to reach a modern road bridge. Turn up steps onto the road and go left back over the main bridge to finish.

Myton Bridge and the River Swale

ON THE URE'S BANK

START *Roecliffe   Grid ref. SE 376659*

DISTANCE *6¹4 miles (10km)*

ORDNANCE SURVEY MAPS
1:50,000
Landranger 99 - Northallerton & Ripon
1:25,000
Explorer 299 - Ripon & Boroughbridge

ACCESS *Start from the village centre. Roadside parking. Served by bus from Harrogate and Knaresborough via Boroughbridge.*

> *Delightful riverside walking close by the Newby Hall estate*

Roecliffe is a very attractive village with houses set back from spacious greens: the red-brick school sits in the middle, sporting a clock tower with a canopied spire and weathervane. There is also a popular pub, the Crown Inn, while St Mary's modest church of 1843 has a small bell turret and a Jacobean pulpit. An enclosed path leaves the village alongside the church, then along a brief track into a farmyard. Turn sharp right to a gate into a welcoming open pasture. Head away left, soon reaching a vantage point revealing the River Ure flowing wide and calm at your feet. Drop to its bank and turn upstream. That is really the last instruction until leaving the river, for the route is never in doubt. A number of stiles, gates and small footbridges are encountered, in a variety of fields and scattered trees, all pretty good stuff.

The river undertakes a steep curve as you pass through Cherry Island Wood, and soon after re-emerging you arrive at Westwick Lock. *Here the short-lived, canalized Westwick Cut helps craft avoid an unnavigable weir just upstream. This is a splendid spot for a break, with the red-brick Lock House alongside: The Island between the two watercourses is popular with anglers. A ferry used to ply the river here.* Resume in the brief company of the dead-straight cut, running by clusters of tall oaks to rejoin the Ure. Top quality rambling continues as Newby Park, the spacious grounds of Newby Hall, occupies the opposite bank. The way runs on through grand sheep pastures. The hall's miniature railway is seen before a classic moment as the house itself suddenly appears, straight across the water and neatly framed by its gardens.

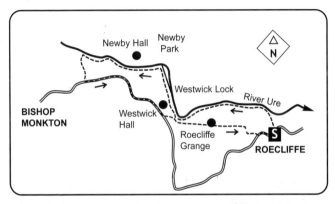

Newby Hall is one of Yorkshire's great stately homes, open to visitors between April and September - though not from this bank of the river! The elegant red-brick house dates from 1705, built for Sir Edward Blackett who made his fortune from collieries on Tyneside. The spacious grounds are an attraction in their own right, comprising some 25 acres of delightful surrounds, also a sculpture park. One or two uncharacteristically moist moments may be encountered before the way enters Holbeck Wood. The path crosses a footbridge on the dead-straight cut of Holbeck, then emerges at a kissing-gate to briefly leave the river. Bear left to meet a surfaced road alongside a couple of sheds. *These nissen huts and concrete bases are the remains of a Second World War military training area that also featured a narrow gauge railway. Alongside is a section of widened river, where engineers erected pontoon bridges which were then tested by tanks.*

Advance briefly along the road to its demise where it bends back left, and keep straight on the rougher road to end in trees at a gate ahead. This next field is your last: look back for a glimpse of the main front of Newby Hall. At the end is a bridge on a side-stream. Don't cross, but take a kissing-gate on the left from where a fieldside path heads away from the river. At the end it becomes a firm, embanked way to emerge back into a field. Again it runs along the side to a gate, then to a small gate onto Boroughbridge Road half a mile east of the edge of Bishop Monkton (see WALK 4).

Turn left to commence a mile on the road, with the early stages occasionally subject to flooding. At the first of two sharp bends by Westwick House Farm the 'Roecliffe $2^3\!4$ miles' sign is mis-leading, as the road takes a more circuitous course; at the second, the access road to Westwick Lock turns off. Just beyond is Westwick Hall Farm, and a minute further a path is signed through a gate on the left. Bear right across the field to look down on the river. The path runs to enter the bridleway of Sheaflands Lane enshrouded in greenery. Turn left on this for a super walk, initially along the top of Cherry Island Wood, with the river just below, then more openly to the farm at Roecliffe Grange. Keep straight on the verges of its access road to emerge onto a road by a nursery. Roecliffe is just a couple of minutes to the left.

Newby Hall

3

COPGROVE

START Burton Leonard   Grid ref. SE 327638

DISTANCE 6$\frac{1}{2}$ miles (10$\frac{1}{2}$km)

ORDNANCE SURVEY MAPS
1:50,000
Landranger 99 - Northallerton & Ripon
1:25,000
Explorer 299 - Ripon & Boroughbridge

ACCESS Start from the village centre. Roadside parking. Served by bus from Ripon, Knaresborough and Harrogate.

> *Three unassuming villages are linked by charming rural ways*

Burton Leonard is a colourful village grouped around an arrangement of greens. St Leonard's church of 1878 stands to one corner, along with a red-brick Methodist church, a village school, the Royal Oak pub, a Post office/shop and the old village pump in a shelter on the lower green. Head east from the centre, past the church and a second pub, the Hare & Hounds, leaving the village on Mill Lane. *From the brow views east look to the Hambleton Hills: visible is the White Horse of Kilburn, along with a much closer and equally celebrated Yorkshire landmark, Ripon Cathedral.*

At a crossroads go straight across and down with a verge, until a turning branches right. Take this, and remain on this access lane to a cattle-grid at the end of a wood. At this path crossroads the access road bears right towards Crow House: your route is straight ahead on a lesser track. Beyond a stile/gate in a fence this improves into a good track, running on past another wood edge to approach a big modern barnyard. While the track swings right to ford Holbeck, you have the option of a footbridge straight ahead.

Now turn right to a gate/stile onto the access road, and go right along it, briefly, passing a pond. Level with Well House, ignore its drive rising away and instead take a gate on the right. Head away outside the wood, holding to the fence on your left to rise pleasantly to a cluster of houses at Copgrove. Advance through a stile and on to a snicket behind, running between hidden gardens to emerge onto an access road, St Mongah's Lane. Go straight ahead on this suburban driveway to emerge at a junction with the through road, alongside a church. *The little church of St Michael & All Angels has a bell-cote and Norman origins.*

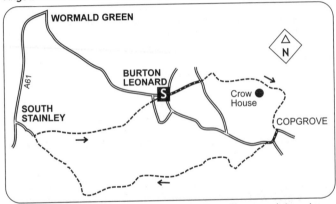

Turn right on the verge, leaving the village and ignoring a branch left at a lodge. The verge leads all the way to your turning, where a surfaced way slants left after a directly ascending drive. This comes just before the road drops to bridge a lake. *It is worth continuing to this point to appraise the splendid large lake which with its swans makes a fine foreground to Copgrove Hall.*

Your side branch, meanwhile, rises outside Dark Walk Wood, improves to a cart track and on to a bridle-gate onto a surfaced access road, Green Lane. Turn right on this, soon reverting to a cart track. The way drops down to Robert Beck in the trees. Don't cross, but take the branch left, which rises away slightly then runs a super course along fieldsides on the southern flank of the beck. A section midway is enclosed by hedgerows to eventually arrive at an access road to Lime Kilns Farm. Keep straight on, rising gently and now largely surfaced to ultimately meet a T-junction. Turn right here, dropping steadily down to run on to the edge of South Stainley. *En route you pass restored Stainley Hall; cross a stone arch bridge on the beck, and conclude through a narrow wooded valley, with the old sandstone quarries of Stainley Gill.* South Stainley is reached at St Wilfrid's church, with its bell-turret. *An old pump stands by the bridge, with the Red Lion pub two minutes further.* Resume by a stile on the right before the church, passing the churchyard to a stile at the end. From here the return to Burton Leonard is largely a straight line. Continue along the hedgeside and on through a gateway in a hedge, continuing to a corner stile alongside a wood.

From a stile at the end keep straight on alongside a hedge, a super green way that runs to meet a firm track coming in from the right. Keep straight on this for a considerable time, largely still with a hedgerow on your left. Ignore a branch left and advance on, dropping to cross a tiny stream in the bottom. Here the track swings right, but is soon left after reaching a hedge rising left. Here a more inviting grassy track ascends the fieldside to a gate into a replanted area. The track climbs steeply through infant trees then resumes on a hedgeside, with the village laid out ahead. Advance all the way to a road, Scarah Lane. Turn left to emerge onto the top of the sloping High Green, descending back into the centre.

St Michael's church, Copgrove

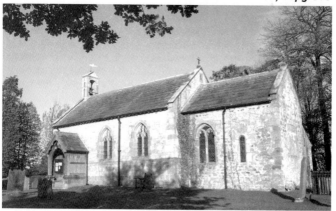

RIPON CANAL

START Bishop Monkton   Grid ref. SE 329662

DISTANCE 6 miles (9¹⁄₂km)

ORDNANCE SURVEY MAPS
1:50,000
Landranger 99 - Northallerton & Ripon
1:25,000
Explorer 299 - Ripon & Boroughbridge

ACCESS Start from the village centre. Roadside parking. Served by bus from Ripon, Knaresborough and Harrogate.

> *The gentle banks of the River Ure lead to a delightful encounter with the towpath of a restored waterway*

Bishop Monkton is a lovely village whose quality features are further enhanced by a lovely stream running through the centre. The church of St John the Baptist boasts a tall spire, and there are two pubs and a shop. Leave by heading south from the Lamb & Flag along the main street in the company of the stream. At the end turn left opposite the Masons Arms, along an enclosed rough lane, Ings Lane. *A modest brow soon affords a brief glimpse of the White Horse of Kilburn, a familiar landmark on the Hambleton Hills beyond the Vale of York.*

Simply remain on its dead straight course all the way past a house and on to a fork: as the main way turns sharp right, keep straight on down a softer track to the bottom just below, where it fades. A leafy enclosed footway takes over, swinging left and running a grand course before emerging into a field. Keep straight on over a stile ahead and along the hedgeside, which terminates just short of a gate onto Boroughbridge Road.

Turn briefly left, and at the village/30mph sign, take a small gate on the right. Head away through a gate and remain on the fieldside, at the corner a firm path takes over and continues along a minor embankment by a stream. This winds along to emerge into another field. *There are glimpses of the red-brick Newby Hall ahead across the currently unseen river (see WALK 2).* At the end the bank of the Ure is gained. Turn left to commence a delightful stretch upstream with the wide flowing river. Initially on an embankment, this soon turns off leaving you to trace the lush bank upstream, soon reaching a major deflection caused by the Ripon Canal. At this pleasant spot the river widely departs, while your path runs to Oxclose Lock just ahead.

The lock was built to convey boats from the Ure onto the two mile long Ripon Canal. This was the northernmost limit of the Ure Navigation, constructed in 1772 to enable river-borne freight to access the city. Its principal import into Ripon was coal, while lead mined in nearby Nidderdale found its way out of the Dales from here. This little waterway was fully abandoned during the mid 20th century after long since losing trade to the railway, but restoration in the 1990s has seen it become a fine addition to Ripon's varied attractions, and a much valued local leisure facility. During the course of World War Two the lock saw military use, for training divers.

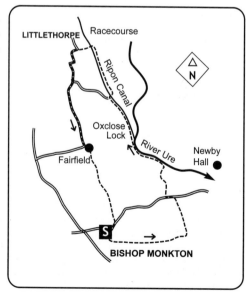

21

A grassy track now heads along the waterside, soon joined by a surfaced access road along to the arch of Rentons Bridge. Cross the bridge and resume on a grassy path along the other bank. *Just over the hedge is Ripon racecourse, while on the other side is Ripon Motor Boat Club.* Next bridge is Nicholsons Bridge, where you leave the canal. Cross it and follow a muddy lane along to a road bend in Littlethorpe. Turn left to a junction by the church. *Red-brick St Michael's church dates from 1878.* Go left on Pottery Lane, passing through the scattered community and a couple of sharp bends, then out past more scattered houses. Beyond them all the road turns sharp right, and here leave it by advancing straight on the left-hand drive in front at Fairfield. To the right is a fishery.

Past a couple of contrasting houses this firm track passes left of a couple of long poultry sheds and away along the fieldside. At a junction at the end go just a few yards left and escape by a stile on the right. Head away along the hedgeside, with Bishop Monkton appearing ahead. A hard track comes in to join you, advance along it swinging left and then on to a couple of isolated sheds. Here the track currently ends. Keep straight on a faint grassy way to a gate/stile ahead. From a stile just beyond, an enclosed path takes over and leads pleasantly back along a fieldside to emerge onto a short drive to enter the village. Go right to finish, past the Mechanics Institution of 1859 and possibly bearing left to conclude alongside the duck-dabbling stream by the neat old Main Street.

A corner of Bishop Monkton

5

RIPON'S RIVERS

START Ripon   Grid ref. SE 312712

DISTANCE 5¼ miles (8½km)

ORDNANCE SURVEY MAPS
1:50,000
Landranger 99 - Northallerton & Ripon
1:25,000
Explorer 299 - Ripon & Boroughbridge

ACCESS Start from the Market Square. Car parks. Served by bus from Leeds, Harrogate, Boroughbridge and York.

> *Very leisurely walking on Ripon's leafy riverbanks*

The smallest of Yorkshire's cities is an outstanding market 'town' dominated by a beautiful Cathedral, the third building on the 7th century site of Wilfrid's monastery. Though destroyed in the 10th century, the Saxon crypt of 672 survives to this day. The present Cathedral dates from the late 12th century, with various additions down the years. The West front presents a stunning high wall filling the end of Kirkgate, while internal delights include the superb east window and a medieval screen. The Market Square is Ripon's buzzing heart, and Thursday markets present an animated scene. Centrepiece is the tall obelisk, whose slender lines replaced an earlier Market Cross in 1702. For many centuries Ripon was under ecclesiastical rule known as 'The Liberty', with the Archbishop of York's authority being greater than that of the King. Under this arrangement a 'Wakeman' was responsible for the townsfolk's safety during the hours of darkness, and this setting of the watch was heralded by the sounding of a horn in the Market Cross, a millennium-old tradition maintained at 9pm each evening.

Overlooking the square is the Town Hall of 1801, originally a town house for the owner of Studley Royal. Less obvious, just doors away, is the Wakeman's House with its Tudor facade. Many of the central street names are still 'gates', and the layout has changed little since medieval times. Apart from the addition of modern suburbs, Ripon's greatest change came as recently as 1996, when rumbling waggons bound for the A1 were finally diverted from its congested streets onto a by-pass. Much of it overlies the former railway, which came to Ripon in the 1840s but was a victim of the Beeching cuts of the 1960s, closing in 1969. Other buildings of interest include Cathedral Hall on the site of a medieval school, with the red-brick Old Hall of 1738 in adjacent Minster Close.

Other varied attractions are the tiny Ripon Canal linked to the River Ure, a waterway only brought back to life in the 1990s: it is the northernmost limit of the national waterway network (see WALK 4). Ripon had a brief flirtation with the spa boom thanks largely to

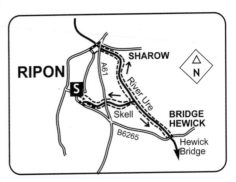

mineral springs discovered at Aldfield, several miles to the west (see WALK 8). Ripon also boasts one of Yorkshire's many famous racecourses, and the Law & Order Museums. In their gaunt Victorian surroundings these consist of three separate sites, the Courthouse, Workhouse and Prison & Police Museum (House of Correction) with its original cells. Guided walks explore varied aspects of Ripon's history, while the Trans-Pennine Way ends its 100-mile journey at this easternmost boundary of the Dales.

From the market place head along Kirkgate to the awesome west front of the cathedral. Bear right along its outer wall, and part way along turn down a firm path, under an arch and out past Cathedral Hall onto High St Agnesgate: turn right. On your left is a Norman arch of the chapel of St Anne's Hospital, an early almshouse, while *Thorp Prebend House is a medieval Canon's house recently restored and open to visitors as a heritage centre.* At the end turn left just as far as Bondgate Bridge on the River Skell. *From here the river makes a fine foreground to the imposing cathedral.*

Across, take steps down to the bank and follow an urban path downstream. This passes a footbridge by the Water Rat pub and onto a road at a ford and footbridge. Continue downstream, now on the road at Fishergreen and soon passing beneath the by-pass for the first time. *The stone arches survive from Ripon's former railway, cynically utilised by modern road builders.* At the end a path takes over, delving into trees to remain true to the Skell to its demise at the confluence with the Ure.

The path turns downstream with the major river, still cloaked in greenery, and though forced up onto an open, grassy flood embankment part way along, this course remains outside the scrubby bank to reach Hewick Bridge. Cross and resume up the east bank. *The Blackamoor pub at Bridge Hewick is just minutes further along the road. Note also, as you get going, the concrete remains of a ford utilized by tanks during Second World War training manouevres. Sharow church tower soon appears on the brow over to the right.* The path retains its course upstream, sometimes through scrub, often on the true wooded bank, and generally very nicely all the way to emerge alongside the Sharow road, without joining it. Instead the path shadows the river under the by-pass and along to the edge of North Bridge, Ripon's major river crossing. Cross and turn left along Magdalen's Road. Just ahead, the Station pub survives long after the railway's demise.

Very quickly, at a bend, pass through an old iron kissing-gate and a path heads off back to the river, again shadowing it under the by-pass and resuming downstream in delightful surrounds to rejoin the Skell. *This stride back to the Skell is the walk's finest section.* The path turns back upstream with Ripon's own river, and though briefly away from it, it runs to a kissing-gate by a house, onto its short drive and back under the by-pass. A suburban street runs on, but at the first chance turn left to meet the Skell once again at the earlier ford and footbridge. Turn up the near side on a suburban path back to the Water Rat. Either cross the bridge to finish as you began, or turn right along the short street to quickly return to the cathedral yard.

MARKENFIELD HALL

START *Markington*   *Grid ref. SE 287649*

DISTANCE *5^{1}2 miles (9km)*

ORDNANCE SURVEY MAPS
1:50,000
Landranger 99 - Northallerton & Ripon
1:25,000
Explorer 298 - Nidderdale
or
Explorer 299 - Ripon & Boroughbridge

ACCESS *Start from the village centre, roadside parking towards the eastern end. The village hall car park may claim local use. Occasional bus service from Ripon.*

> *A mild-mannered country ramble built around the highlight of a close encounter with a magnificent old building*

Markington is an attractive street village boasting two pubs, a Post office/shop and the 19th century church of St Michael the Archangel. From the village hall go west along the main street past the Yorkshire Hussar, and turn right on the Fountains Abbey road. Immediately after crossing Markington Beck bear right on a drive to a lone house, past which a kissing-gate admits to sports fields. Bear left past the pavilion, past the cricket pitch and keep left to find a path departing up a low bank behind goalposts. A thin path heads diagonally away along the right side of a hedge. From a gate at the end head away in nicer surrounds, picking up a faint green track which runs pleasantly along the fieldside to the houses at Waterloo.

Pass along the front of the buildings but without setting foot on the road, turn left up a short snicket to a stile into deep undergrowth. The path rises as a superb, hollowed way through wood-land, and along to emerge onto a narrow road. *Just up to the left is the impressive frontage of Ingerthorpe Hall.* The route goes right a few steps to take an old stile in the wall, crossing the field to approach the farm at Yarrows Hill, ahead. *Over to the right the Hambleton Hills form a distant skyline.* On the edge of the yard, keep left of all buildings and rise left to a gate. Bear right along the hedgeside to a corner stile onto a junction of tracks between new plantations. Keep straight on a grassy track to reach a stile into further plantings. Advance just a few steps and bear left on a grassy track to a wooded bank, then continue along its foot to a corner stile admitting onto the narrow course of Strait Lane.

Turning left, this slender bridleway immediately emerges into a field. Head away along the hedges of two fieldsides, with the tall spire of Studley Royal directly ahead. *You can savour spacious views over the last of this rolling country falling to the Vale of Mowbray. To the left behind Morcar House Farm is a prominent tower on the distinctive knoll of How Hill. In the care of the National Trust, the tower replaced a chapel known as Michael-how-Hill built by Abbot Marmaduke Huby of Fountains Abbey.*

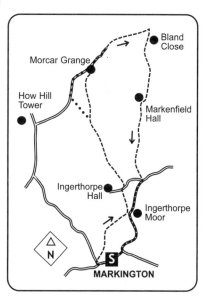

At the field corner, with Studley Royal church spire directly ahead and Morcar House Farm just to the left, bridle-gates lead on through two fields. Advancing on to a hedge corner, bear right across a ploughed field to another bridle-gate. Go left along the hedgeside, and at the end a choice awaits. The farmer's preferred alter-native route (avoiding a farmyard) passes through the gap in the very corner to advance pleasantly along the fieldside to a gate onto Whitcliffe Lane, where turn right to Morcar Grange Farm. The right of way uses the gate just a few steps to the right, bearing right over a modest brow. From here you can absorb a particularly strong sense of space, with a substantial moorland skyline to the left, and the distant line of the North York Moors to the right: How Hill chapel and Studley spire also feature. Descend through a gate and cross to Morcar Grange, emerging through the often muddy yard onto Whitcliffe Lane.

Turn right along the narrow road. *On your right is a large pond, while far ahead a long skyline of the Hambleton Hills features a very distinctive White Horse of Kilburn*. This remains your way for some time, soon losing its surface as it runs through an archetypal rolling landscape. Eventually rising to meet a narrow lane on a brow, turn right. *First though, glance down to the left to see the city of Ripon: sat uneasily amidst its small community is the Cathedral, its mellow stone partly obscured when trees are in full summer greenery*. The drive runs to the large farm at Bland Close, but from the cattle-grid remain on the hedgeside, through the fields to rise to the brow ahead. On the brow, advance just as far as the end of the wood on the right, where an old stile in the old park wall leads into the corner of a large field. Positioned ahead is the very imposing silhouette of Markenfield Hall. Rise towards it, keeping left to a stile/gate alongside. This is a stupendous moment, as it runs by the hall to reveal its moated splendour. *Note also from this side the great east window of the chapel.*

Markenfield Hall is a fortified manor house dating from 1310. Long-time home of the Markenfield family, Sir Thomas saw an end to that when he played a major role in the Rising of the North in 1569: when this floundered the estate was forfeited, eventually passing to Lord Grantley. Another member of the family, Sir Ninian Markenfield, fought at Flodden Field in 1513. A chapel in Ripon Cathedral recalls the family with fine 14th and 15th century tombs.

Emerging via a stile onto its drive, turn right to the entrance to the hall, and gaze with awe at the magnificent scene. *Fronted by a working farm, this is still very much a home. In front is the 16th century gatehouse guarding the bridge over the moat. The hall is open to the fee-paying public on a limited basis, currently afternoons daily in early May and late June. Happily much can be seen from outside, but it is certainly worth a fuller appraisal if arriving on the right day. The excellently preserved interior includes a fine banqueting hall and the chapel, a good deal of restoration having taken place in recent times.*

Back on the drive go left between 18th century outbuildings, and as it turns left, advance a few yards right then take a gate on the left before a set of pens. Head across the fields on a splendid green track. A short enclosed section precedes a final field, where bear right to a stile back onto Strait Lane, at the other end of its narrow section. Here go left along its broad beginnings, absorbing a broader track to emerge onto a road. Turn right, and if not taking the immediate lane right to return by the outward route, remain on this road past extensive Ingerthorpe Moor Farm and Waterloo to return to the village. Markington Beck is re-crossed in a lovely setting, deep in woodland where snowdrops proliferate. The road climbs past the grounds of Markington Hall to re-enter the village. *Two great wings protrude at this 17th century manor house featuring numerous mullioned windows.* Turn right along the road, appraising the hall and passing the Cross Keys to conclude.

The gatehouse, Markenfield Hall

7

FOUNTAINS ABBEY

START *Fountains Abbey*   *Grid ref. SE 272686*

DISTANCE *5 miles (8km)*

ORDNANCE SURVEY MAPS
1:50,000
Landranger 99 - Northallerton & Ripon
1:25,000
Explorer 298 - Nidderdale **or**
Explorer 299 - Ripon & Boroughbridge

ACCESS *Start from the National Trust Visitor Centre off the B6265 Pateley Bridge-Ripon road, almost 3 miles west of Ripon. Served by buses from Ripon. There is an appreciable (though worth every penny) entry fee to the Abbey for non-National Trust members. Open daily from 10am, except Christmas Eve, Christmas Day, and Fridays in January, November and December.*

> *Unparalleled beauty awaits in this sumptuous promenade around a designated World Heritage Site. Fountains Abbey and Studley Royal offer a stunning combination of majestic ruins, exquisite water gardens and spacious deer park. Though the walk isn't demanding, don't pencil this in for a half-day!*

Leaving the visitor centre the surfaced path immediately forks: take the right branch, curving through trees then out into an open pasture - revealing a first view of the abbey tower - to a gate into a wooded bank. Take the left branch down to the abbey. *Set forth to explore the delights of this staggeringly beautiful ruin, the most extensive Cistercian remains in England. Fountains Abbey was founded in 1132 by a group of dissatisfied Benedictine monks from St Mary's Abbey in York: seeking a stricter routine they turned to the French Cistercian order. Though it would have been a much wilder place then, the setting they chose could be matched only by perhaps Bolton and Rievaulx. Built largely between the mid 12th and 13th centuries, this was one of the most important religious houses. Whilst their granges occupied much of nearby Nidderdale, their possessions stretched to the Cumberland fells. Dairy farming, lead mining and other industry also came within their scope: many ordinary peoples' lives revolved around the abbey. Perhaps the abbey's finest feature is the 300ft long west range, the remarkable vaulted cellarium. Most impressive is the 180ft high tower, a 16th century addition built by Abbot Marmaduke Huby: it remained incomplete at the Dissolution.*

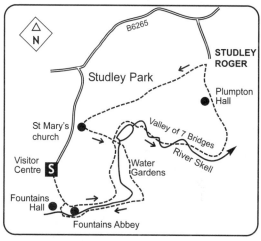

Rejoining the main carriageway, scars on the left show evidence of quarrying for the great building programme. Surfaced throughout, the drive provides a smashing walk along to the water gardens, regarded, once again, as the finest in the country. *Since the Trust's takeover of the estate in the early 1980s, these superb gardens have been subject to an extensive restoration programme, and once again resemble the beautiful scene created throughout the 1700s by the new owners, the Aislabie family. All the buildings such as the temples and the Octagon Tower were added during this period.*

Beyond a bend above Half Moon Pond, running above the canalised Skell you are treated to views over the Moon Pond, flanked by crescents and with lead statues in attendance, to the Temple of Piety: high above, meanwhile, are other features for the return journey. At the eastern end of the grounds another shop sees you out past a ticket office to emerge at the lake and the Studley Royal deer park. *Here also is a tearoom and WC.*

Follow the drive alongside the lake, and at the end remain with the lake on a track to the outflow. Here begins the walk through the Valley of Seven Bridges, the first being a wooden one over the outflow. *Look back from here to see the spire of St Mary's church silhouetted high above the deer park.* The Skell is accompanied downstream through this steep sided valley, a delightful amble that re-crosses the river on five further occasions by means of identical stone arched bridges. After the last one the estate is vacated, temporarily, at a tall kissing-gate, and a woodland path runs down to pass the seventh bridge (this plain structure is not crossed) before the track climbs the wooded bank to leave the river. Out of the trees it runs a pleasant fieldside course with open views. *Most remarkable aspect is the immediate appearance of Ripon Cathedral little more than a stone's throw away, with a long line of the Hambleton Hills beyond.*

Passing mellow-walled Plumpton Hall and its farm buildings, the track becomes surfaced to reach the edge of Studley Roger at a lodge and a small green. *This little village features attractive cottages with red pantile roofs. Look right along the carriageway which forms a perfect alignment with the cathedral and the church.* Go left on the estate drive, through the East Entrance arch to re-enter the park. Strolling along the broad driveway, St Mary's church is framed beyond the long avenue of limes. *In the heart of the centuries-old deer park many of these creatures can be seen, with Red, Fallow (most numerous) and Sika deer all present.*

When cars are sent left to the car park above the lake, either go with them, or incorporate a visit to the church by remaining on the drive. *St Mary's was built in 1871-78, boasting an impressive great spire prominent in many views around the neighbourhood. It is open on afternoons from Easter to October. A tall obelisk of 1815 stands just behind the church.* From the church a grassy path descends to the east entrance to the abbey by the lake.

Re-entering, turn left and cross the Skell as it enters the lake, either by footbridge or stepping-stones. The path heads back past the water gardens, but just before reaching the Temple of Piety, a high-level alternative offers itself. Doubling back up, pass through the dark-walled Serpentine Tunnel to emerge by the Octagon Tower. *This provides good views over the smaller Half Moon Pond and much of the grounds, including the Banqueting Hall opposite, and the church spire.* Continuing, the broad path runs on past the Temple of Fame to Surprise View at Ann Boleyn's Seat. *The surprise at this wooden shelter is the sudden return of the abbey to the scene, in dramatic style beyond a sharp bend of the river.* Just past here the path doubles back down the wooded bank to rejoin the lower one at Half Moon Pond. Turning left the way runs on by the river to return to the abbey, passing Robin Hood's Well en route. One can turn down to the start of the ruins for further exploration, or remain on the path above the abbey to arrive at the old abbey mill. Here the path returns to join the main carriageway.

Along to the left is Fountains Hall. With its intricate facade this magnificent house was completed in 1611, much of the stone being plundered from the abbey that had only been abandoned in 1539. Last private owners were the Vyner family, descendants of the Aislabies, and much evidence of their presence is found here - note a particularly touching memorial in the hall entrance stairway. Return to the starting point by following the surfaced path up the wooded bank.

**St Mary's church,
Studley Royal**

ALDFIELD SPA

START *Fountains Bridge*   *Grid ref. SE 270681*

DISTANCE *6 miles (9½km)*

ORDNANCE SURVEY MAPS
1:50,000
Landranger 99 - Northallerton & Ripon
1:25,000
Explorer 298 - Nidderdale

ACCESS *Start from the Fountains Abbey West Gate car park at Fountains Bridge. This is disabled priority parking, so please park towards the rear. Occasional bus from Ripon.*

> *A pilgrimage to a largely forgotten sulphur well precedes a splendid ramble around the deer parks of Studley Royal*

While this walk explores the outer sections of Studley Royal and offers good views of the abbey and its surroundings, it does not enter the central section (fee payable) which is visited in WALK 7. From the car park walk to the bridge, over which is the West Gate entrance to the estate beneath the imposing Fountains Hall. *Until the construction of the visitor centre, this was the main entrance to Fountains. Alongside are the former Abbey Stores, only a Victorian postbox survives.* Head away along the road as far as a sharp bend, and take a stile in front. A grassy cart track heads away, dropping down to shadow the tinkling beck of the River Skell.

Advance into the woods alongside an impressive three-arched bridge. Also ignoring any small bridges on the Skell, the track runs unfailingly on for a good mile, a super walk through Skell Bank and Spa Gill Woods. Entering an extensive clearing, the Skell is now some distance away. Further, as the trees close in again, a ruin is reached. Heavily cloaked in undergrowth, this once substantial building was linked with Aldfield Spa. Though your path turns off here, first advance twenty strides beyond the ruin, where a slim path runs left to a footbridge on the Skell. Immediately across is a humble, brick-lined well with the once celebrated water bubbling up. *Both smell and taste quickly confirm its sulphurous nature. The mineral springs were discovered in the late 17th century, and contributed greatly towards Ripon's efforts at being a spa town.*

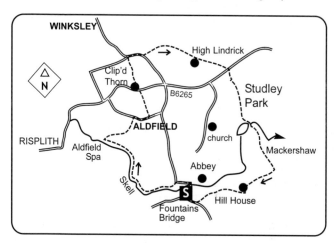

Back at the ruin take the grassy way up its near side, then immediately take a slimmer branch right. This rises a few steps and doubles back more clearly to the right to run a level course before gradually ascending the bank. A stile at the top puts you into a pasture, and a grooved way heads off. As this fades, rise left and cross to a gate: ahead are the scattered houses of Aldfield. Cross to another gate ahead, and on again to a small iron gate onto the road. Path and map are not quite in unison here, to the west of Spa Ghyll Farm. Turn right along the footway, just as far as a phone box outside a former chapel. *Further along the street is St Laurence's church, dating from the 1780s and featuring a three-decker pulpit and box pews.*

From a gate on the left, cross to a stile into a sliver of wood-land. Out the other side head away with the hedge on your left, and keep on to the far end where a stile awaits in the facing fence. Aim for the solitary house at Clip'd Thorn, to find a gate onto the B6265 in front of it. Go right a few steps to a stile sending you down the side of the outer garden to a small gate into a vast field. Descend to the bottom, guided by a tall hedgerow to find a ladder-stile into the garden at North House. Pass through the orchard left of the house, down into a rough enclosure to a stile at the bottom right corner. *Ahead to the left is an impressive moorland skyline, with Winksley church tower prominent just across the valley of the River Laver.* Entering another large field, descend to the bottom right corner and a stile into woodland.

A potentially gruesome few minutes await, as the faint path can be choked by undergrowth in late summer. A path does exist however, steadily descending a largely straight line to debouch not a moment too soon onto a back road. Ignoring a junction just yards to the left, turn right for a five minute spell still in woodland, and just before the trees on the right end, bear off left on a roughly surfaced road. This transforms into a cart track running to meet a T-junction at the wood corner. Turn right, and this same track leads on to approach High Lindrick. Remain on the broadening track, left of farm buildings to meet the access road a little further. *Studley Royal church spire rises ahead, while to the left a long skyline of the Hambleton Hills features the White Horse of Kilburn.* The drive runs back out onto the B6265.

In front is the tall estate wall of Studley Royal, with some imposing entrance gates to the left. These are firmly locked, but cross and go a few strides right to find a little door set into the wall. This lets you into the park, which is Open Access land. Either go left to join the surfaced carriageway, or advance further on before turning to join it a little further. It rises to a brow to reveal Studley Royal House to your right, and Ripon's glowing cathedral far to the left. *The house has been created from the stables of the original Studley Royal, which was destroyed by fire in 1946. It is unthinkable that you will not encounter some of the hundreds of deer that roam this centuries-old deer park, the three breeds present being Red deer, Fallow deer (most numerous) and Sika deer, introduced from Manchuria in the 1600s.*

The direct route simply remains on the verges of the carriage-way down to a crossroads with a long avenue perfectly aligned with Ripon Cathedral and the church, then down again to approach the Lake. *To visit Studley Royal church, bear right on a splendid grassy path immediately after the branch to the house, contouring unfailingly towards the church. St Mary's was built in 1871-78, boasting an impressive great spire prominent in many views around the neighbourhood. It is open on afternoons from Easter to October. From the church a grassy path descends to the east entrance to the abbey by the lake.* At whatever point the lake is reached, bear left to its outflow.

Cross the wooden footbridge into the head of the Valley of Seven Bridges (see WALK 7). Across, ignore the path running into the grassy valley, instead remain on the cart track which quickly slants up the wooded bank. A tall gate admits into the higher-level rolling pasture of Mackershaw. *This delightful area is also Open Access, and is regularly frequented by deer.* The grassy track rises away left, but as it climbs above a pond towards a gate, bear right on a fainter way. This maintains a delightful climb, past another pond and along to a hugely imposing gateway at the remains of Mackershaw Lodge. *A mid-18th century 'eyecatcher' to be viewed from Studley Royal, it was occupied into the 1960s, and now awaits restoration.*

Through the gate a bridle-path is joined. Turn right through woodland to emerge into an open pasture. Rise directly away to a hedge corner and along to the farm at Hill House. Keep left to join the access road, then bear right towards the house. Just before it branch left to a gate and stone bridge out into a field. Double sharply back right on a grassy track running to a gate at the end. *En route admire the well-sited farmhouse across the beck.* Just a little further bear left on an enclosed way, and from a gate at the end advance on, with the old park wall to your left. *Quickly revealed ahead is Fountains Hall in dense woodland, and a little further Huby's tower at the abbey dramatically appears: this brow offers splendid views of the abbey's environs.* Simply keep straight on the faint track, passing a small pond and on to a gate at the end. Joining a back road, turn right. *Almost at once you quickly gain an even better prospect of the facade of the hall.* The road drops to a T-junction, with the start point just down to the right.

9

EAVESTONE LAKE

START Sawley   Grid ref. SE 248677

DISTANCE 5 miles (8km)

ORDNANCE SURVEY MAPS
1:50,000
Landranger 99 - Northallerton & Ripon
1:25,000
Explorer 298 - Nidderdale

ACCESS Start from the expansive green-cum-playing fields. Ample car parking alongside. Occasional bus from Ripon.

> Charming rolling estate country leads by a string of historic features to the lovely wooded lakes of Eavestone

Sawley is a small but outwardly affluent village in the estate country west of Fountains Abbey. The tiny church of St Michael & All Angels dates from 1879, on the site of a chapel built by Archbishop Huby of Fountains Abbey. A bell remains in place on a former schoolhouse at the top of the green, at the bottom of which is the Parish Room of 1900. Village pub is the Sawley Arms.

From the green walk back through the village between the church and the pub to a T-junction. From a stile in the facing wall head away across the field, bearing gently away from the road over to the left. From a gate/stile at the other side, head away with a hedge on the left, at the far end joining a driveway through the fields. Bear right on this to a cattle-grid at the entrance to Lacon Hall. *Lacon Hall's mullioned windows form part of an attractive frontage dating from the 16th century: it replaced a timber hall of the once important Lacon family.* Heeding a path diversion, don't enter but turn right along the fieldside to the corner. Bear left to another corner, slanting gently away from the grounds, through a line of scrub, and on to a wall ahead. Turn up its near side to a plantation at the top. *This faint path shows signs of causeying, being distinctly raised in parts and therefore clearly of some age and former importance.*

Look back for a view of the hall, and far across the Vale of Mowbray to the Hambleton Hills. From a stile at the top corner cross diagonally to a similar corner, passing close by Lacon Cross. *This wayside cross on its solid base is hollowed at the top, and dates from monastic times, when it was astride a route west from Fountains Abbey towards Nidderdale.* At the corner a stile admits onto well-named Green Lane. Go right to emerge into a vast field. A near-comprehensive surround of plantations proves surprisingly non-claustrophobic. Aim across the field, bearing right of the one visible farmhouse amid green fields opposite. Locate a small gate admitting to the plantation in front, alongside an elaborate spring.

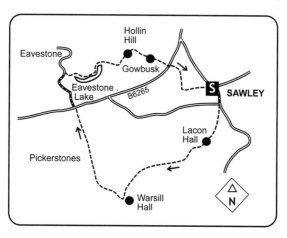

A broad track slants down to the right, but leave it almost at once by a path dropping left off it. This descends a steep wooded bank to a forest road, crossing straight over to immediately cross the ancient and overgrown Butterton Bridge on Picking Gill. *The stone-arched bridge is yet more evidence of this centuries-old*

route. A grassy cart track continues away from the beck above a smaller side beck. As it swings steeply left uphill, advance straight on a path, keeping company with the sidestream. This splendid sunken way rises below a collapsed wall before reaching another gate out of the woods. Rise to a gateway above, then head up the fieldside to a gate at the top corner. From it head away to locate a wall-stile to the right of the farm buildings of Warsill Hall.

Turn right on a wallside track towards impending plantations. Through a gate near a plantation corner on the left, the track crosses a field centre to the next gate, with the realisation that the great swathes of plantation must surely envelop you before long! *Back to the right the Hambleton Hills skyline seems only a stone's throw away.* Another wallside leads on to the right-hand of two gates, into a plantation corner. The map falsely suggests this last field on the left is also a plantation. The grand enclosed way runs inside the plantation boundary to join the bend of a forest road.

Advance directly along this, running straight as a die through the heart of the plantation of High Moor. Ignoring any branches - including the main track's swing to the left - it rises gently to leave the plantation at a gate. A green track then runs on outside the boundary wall, soon leaving the trees behind completely. *Big views return, with Kirkby Malzeard Moor prominent on the skyline over to the left.* Dropping down to a gate onto the B6265 Pateley Bridge-Ripon road, cross straight over and down the Eavestone cul-de-sac.

Down past the farm, as the road swings sharply left, descend a little then take a path doubling back into the wood. Here begins a glorious spell on a brilliant path in magnificent surroundings. First feature is the upper reservoir above Eavestone Lake, with a dark crag jutting out into the water. *The gritstone surrounding these two lakes is a goldmine for rock climbers, a late developer as a climbing ground but now yielding climbs of every standard on at least sixteen separate buttresses: some of these literally overhang your path by the main lake!* Crossing its outflow the path winds round to the head of Eavestone Lake, along which it runs the full length. *Of immediate interest are the forbidding outcrops of Ravens Crag towering, often in shadow, above the opposite bank. Abundant waterfowl, springtime bluebells and wild garlic amid the luxuriant foliage of this mixed woodland combine to provide a half-hour of sheer delight.*

At the end fork right to cross a small dam and a lovely little arched bridge. Penance rears its head in the form of a sustained direct pull through Fishpond Wood. A gate at the top consigns the Eavestone scene to memory, as you pass round the left side of a field to join the drive to Hollin Hill Farm. Take its drive round to the back, and go straight on through a gate into a scrubby corner. Advance into the field corner, and keep to the right to quickly find a ladder-stile into a slim enclosure. As it opens out keep with its right side to run along to West Gowbusk. Go straight through the farmyard and out along the drive, but quickly leave by a private-looking gate on the left. This accesses the front of a cottage at Gowbusk, to follow its drive out onto the B6265. Go briefly left and take a stile on the right: the houses of Sawley appear ahead.

Cross the field to a stile in the far corner, then rise gently along the fieldsides. *Broad views look across to the North York Moors; note also the prominent spire of Studley Royal church and perhaps a glimpse of the tower of Fountains Abbey itself in the intervening rolling country.* Entering a rough enclosed lane, leave at once by a stile on the left and descend the fieldside. A stile at the bottom admits to a short-lived hedgerowed green path. A stile at the end sends you down fieldsides to re-enter the village green by way of a wall-stile.

Lacon Cross

✓ DALLOWGILL

START *Dallowgill Moor*   *Grid ref. SE 199707*

DISTANCE *7 miles (11km)*

ORDNANCE SURVEY MAPS
1:50,000
Landranger 99 - Northallerton & Ripon
1:25,000
Explorer 298 - Nidderdale

ACCESS *Start from the Grantley road junction on Dallowgill Moor, a short half-mile before the Pateley Bridge to Kirkby Malzeard road crosses a cattle-grid to leave the moor south of the Drovers Inn. Parking just north of the junction alongside a tall boundary stone, with more space by the junction itself.*

> *A super walk in a quiet valley on the fringe of sweeping moorland, with the added novelty of a mosaic trail*

Just north of the road junction a footpath is signed off to the left, and a grassy way slants down the moor. *From the outset you can enjoy a grand prospect over Dallowgill's rolling pastoral landscape richly interspersed with woodland beneath sweeping moorland.* Although intermittent at times the way points down to a corner of the moor where a stile in a gate awaits. Head straight down the field, a wall forming to lead down to a gate onto the unsurfaced access road to Dallow.

Turn left into the hamlet, passing a short row of cottages to emerge into the open just short of a plantation. As the access track swings up to the left, advance straight on a nicer green way outside the top of the plantation. *Here you might espy a mosaic inside the wood, the first of at least ten that the walk encounters.*

The trail was created in 1997, and each of 22 colourful mosaics carries an individual local scene, most commonly of wildlife. Locations on this walk are indicated thus (•). The track enters the trees a little further along to descend steeply to South Gill.

Cross by a footbridge at a setted ford, then turn right (•) on a broader track to cross the larger North Gill. *Their confluence creates the River Laver.* The forest road now climbs steeply right, leaving the trees. As it swings sharp right towards the road, take a stile on the left (•) and cross the field to a gate into the woods (•). A superb grassy path runs along the top of this oakwood, enjoying delightful bluebell surrounds in springtime. The path ceases at a bridle-gate at the far end. Now below Grey Green Farm, continue along the wallside through the fields to Bents House (•), and on across two further fields to buildings ahead. At this long derelict farm turn right up its grassy drive to rise onto a moorland road.

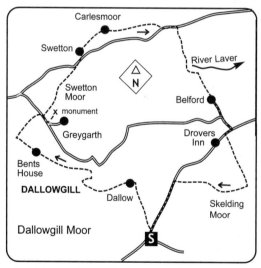

Go right to the cattle-grid, and while the route turns up the near side onto the moor, first make the tiny detour over the grid to a junction with the lane to Dallowgill Methodist Chapel. A stile and signpost on the left send a thin path up a stony pasture to

Greygarth Monument. *Erected to commemorate Queen Victoria's Diamond Jubilee in 1897, it was restored in 1984. Inside, a ladder leads to a viewing platform. This outstanding vantage point reveals great sweeps of moorland, from those you are fringing to the distant line of the Hambleton and Cleveland Hills of the North York Moors on the eastern horizon. Northernmost of these is the prominent peak of Roseberry Topping, diminutive but unmistakable. At your feet is the cluster of buildings of Greygarth in the midst of mile upon mile of pastoral country richly interspersed with woodland.*

Although your onward route could logically be joined by crossing the stony terrain to a gate in the wall opposite, there is no official path to let you do this. So, the good guys will retrace steps to the cattle-grid back onto the moor. Turn up onto the moorland on the right, rising by the wall to the top of Greygarth Hill (951ft/290m). *Now just over the wall from the monument, this is the same superb vantage point.* Advance further to descend with the wall, and when it turns away bear gently left down through the heather and rough grass of Swetton Moor to rejoin the road.

Drop down the verge to a cattle-grid, and just beyond turn down a farm drive to Swetton on the left. Level with the house, go right down a delightful side garden to a gate admitting to the top corner of a plantation. A path heads away, dropping pleasantly to cross Carlesmoor Beck by a wooden footbridge. Rising half-right up the wooded bank a path leaves the trees at a stile to join a track just yards above. Turn right in front of the farm buildings and along the rough lane (•). *Passing The Grange, note the stone above the doorway carved with the names of Henry Robinson & Elizabeth AD 1793.*

Approaching the scattered grouping of Carlesmoor, bear right down an access road for a long, pleasant stride (•). *A three-arched aqueduct hides in trees to the right.* A stream provides company before the lane eventually rises onto the road you left earlier (•). *Note the mis-spelt 'Carlsmoor' sign, and open views to the south over Carlesmoor Beck.* Go left up to the brow (•) and then branch right, descending a hedgerowed way to a ford and footbridge on Carlesmoor Beck. *This tranquil corner is one to linger over: note the notched gatepost immediately over the bridge, and the abundance of holly.* Rising less claustrophobically to a junction of green ways (•), go left through a gate to descend towards the beck. However a sharp turn right (•) sees you on your way again, encountering a section of stone causey en route to another ford and footbridge, this time over the youthful River Laver in similarly delightful circumstances.

A steep climb past Low Belford quickly becoming surfaced to rise onto the road to Dallowgill (•). Head straight up this to meet the Pateley Bridge-Kirkby Malzeard road just below the Drovers Inn. *This landmark pub stands on the edge of the moorland road to Pateley Bridge in Nidderdale: it is normally closed out of season midweek lunchtimes.* Just yards before the pub turn left up the grassy bridleway of Westhod Lane, which ascends gradually and delectably before running along to a corner of Skelding Moor. Through the gate turn immediately right along the moor edge on a reasonable way, and at the end keep straight on through a gate and across a field. Bear right at the end to a gate in the far wall to return to a colourful corner of the open moor. Bear right, remaining near the wall which curves around, later finding a little path forming in the heather to meet the moor road by a cattle-grid. The start point is just a few easy minutes up the verge.

The Drovers Inn, Dallowgill

11

THROPE EDGE

START *Pott Ridge*   *Grid ref. SE 143779*

DISTANCE *7½ miles (12km)*

ORDNANCE SURVEY MAPS
1:50,000
Landranger 99 - Northallerton & Ripon
1:25,000
Explorer 298 - Nidderdale

ACCESS *Start from a cattle-grid where Pott Moor High Road enters the open moor a mile west of Leighton Reservoir at the top of Pott Bank. Small parking area, without blocking access. Alternative parking area half a mile west (on the route) where the footpath leaves the road. • OPEN ACCESS (Jenny Twigg detour) see page 8.*

A memorable stride almost entirely on moorland ways, visiting the delectable upper reaches of neighbouring Nidderdale

From the very outset this walk enjoys massive views: both Leighton and Roundhill reservoirs are hidden as moorland entirely dominates the scene. From the cattle-grid head west along the moor-edge road for a good half-mile, reaching a parking area where an inviting grassy track branches off right. *A splendid stone guidepost (see page 3) is inscribed with the names of Masham, Lofthouse, New Houses and Kettlewell: the old grassy track heads towards the latter two, New Houses being a Nidderdale farm, and Kettlewell much further over a second watershed, in Wharfedale.* Head off up this track, which makes a long, very steady ascent over Pott Moor. *Look back to see Teesside, the plains, Roseberry Topping and the Cleveland and Hambleton Hills.* Alongside a wall ignore a shooters' track branching right, and maintain a super stride on this super track, all the way up through the heather to eventually arrive at a gate by a wall corner. *Thirty paces to the right stands a wall-side boundary stone, inscribed 'Mashamshire' and 'Fountains Earth'.*

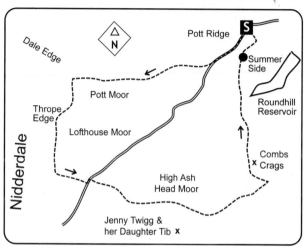

Passing through the gate, it is but a minute further along the wallside to the brow. An unmarked stone is passed at the high point of the track, and within a further minute a crossroads of green ways is reached at a gate. *Alongside is an inscribed stone long since weathered illegible.* At your feet is a stunning prospect of Upper Nidderdale, now also featuring Scar House Reservoir and a host of farms and features beneath the moors. While your old track drops down to the farms on The Edge, the route now turns left on the track encircling Nidderdale, as it moves from Dale Edge to Thrope Edge. *The views along the dale rank superlatives: a fine contrast is formed by the green of the valley at your feet and the dark outlines of rounded Meugher, Great Whernside and Little Whernside on the western skyline.*

Beyond a slight rise to the walk's high point at 1444ft/440m on Lofthouse Moor, the way drops down past some scattered rocks. *Further boulders just to the right make this the finest place to take a break - Greenhow Hill and Menwith Hill are seen way down the valley.* Revealed in the dip just ahead is the shooting house on Thrope Edge. *From the valley road far below this appears as a church silhouetted on the skyline.* Continue past this on the access track past a minor edge, then quickly swinging away left with a wall to lose the intimate Nidderdale scene, and running along the moor edge all the way down to a gate onto Pott Moor High Road.

Turn left for a minute then bear right along a rougher surfaced road. *Here stands another illegible old milestone.* The walled lane runs to a gate onto Longside Moor, then continues as a wallside track to soon reach a fork. Bear left over open moor, rising slightly to the next gate. Again a wall provides company, soon reaching a stone shooting cabin over the wall. At this point the great boulders of Jenny Twigg and her Daughter Tib are seen through the gate. *Assuming access land is open (and you've no dog), then through the gate a grassy shooters' track heads down past a line of butts, from where cross to gain the stones. This giant pair are splendid land-marks, the daughter being little short of her mother in stature.*

The onward route resumes along the track to a major junction at a boundary stone. *By now you have a sweeping vista over the Kirkby Malzeard moors to the Vale of Mowbray, backed by Teesside and the North York Moors, featuring Roseberry Topping, the Cleveland and Hambleton Hills, and also the Yorkshire Wolds.* Keep straight on the main track a few minutes further to a slightly rougher descent. *Part way down, the boulders of Combs Crags are seen to the left, as well as distant Leighton Reservoir.* On briefly levelling out, double back left on a hugely inviting grassy track which quickly reveals, and equally quickly arrives at, Combs Crags.

Ample scrambling opportunities are available, while a pair of stone shooters' cabins sit in their shelter. As the track abruptly ends, you now commence a few minutes of gentle heather bashing. The right of way is invisible on the ground, so simply maintain the same line as you slant down through the heather of Low Ash Head Moor in line with the dwindling boulders to your right. The ground drops away a little more to reveal a couple of derelict farms in the side valley of Agill (the head of Pott Valley) below. Your objective is the less preserved right-hand farm, Low Ash Head.

Slant right down to a stile in a contouring fence near a wall corner, then down the wallside to a corner gate off the moor. Drop left through a gate and then cross to the old farm. Pass round the back and drop down the field to a wall-stile below, then slant right above the colourful sidestream, past a wall corner and down to join a track. Follow this left over the stream and through a gate into the trees, bridging the major stream and then climbing out the other side. Keep to the wall on your right to locate, 50 yards short of a gate above, a wall-stile part hidden by a small holly. Now slant across a large sloping pasture (with West Summer Side Farm just above), locating a wall-stile higher up the other side.

Slant across to a gate where a tiny section of wall and fence meet. Though the easiest way passes through the gate and up to the top corner gate, the map suggests you rise with the fence to a small gate in the top of it. Just a few yards further along the wall-side pass through a gate in it, then turn right and on through an old wall alongside the scant ruins of Summer Side. Just beyond, a clear track (the direct route) is joined at the ruins. Turn up this past a stone shed, and through the gate turn right along the wallside. *Nice views look over Roundhill Reservoir to the moors.* At the far end pass through a gate alongside derelict buildings and a bungalow at East Summer Side, then leave the access track by slanting left across the field, locating a stile in the opposite wall. One further, smaller field is crossed to a gate onto the road by the cattle-grid.

Thrope Edge

ILTON MOOR

START Leighton   Grid ref. SE 156787

DISTANCE 9 miles (14$\frac{1}{2}$km)

ORDNANCE SURVEY MAPS
1:50,000
Landranger 99 - Northallerton & Ripon
1:25,000
Explorer 298 - Nidderdale

ACCESS Start from a lay-by just west of the anglers' car park at
Leighton Reservoir ('P' on the map refers to the anglers' car park).

> *A memorable stride through the heather above a lovely
> side valley, rounded off by a visit to a remarkable folly*

Leighton Reservoir was constructed by Leeds Corporation
early in the 20th century, and is a popular venue for fly fishing.
Across the water rise the purple moors that will soon be underfoot. A curiously shaped tower is a sighting tower, one of several
erected to aid construction of the aqueduct carrying water to the
West Riding's taps. Heading west along the road, it immediately
bridges a finger of the upper reservoir then continues along the
shore. As it swings up Pott Bank, bear left over a cattle-grid on a
surfaced access road. *Just above on the through road, Pott Hall
Farm operates as Island Heritage, where rare breeds of sheep are
raised to produce woollen goods.* Your side road crosses the fields
to Roundhill House. *This is the former reservoir keeper's house of
1903.* The continuing road runs along the top of the masonry dam
of Roundhill Reservoir. *Pre-dating its neighbour, this was built by
Harrogate Corporation. Both dams were supplied with materials
by a narrow gauge tramway from the branch line at Masham.*

Immediately across, vacate the main track and opt for the left-hand gate. A track rises up the rough pasture to a track junction in front of a fence. Turn right to a gate in the wall, from where a grassy track ascends to a gate (with an in-built stile) onto Arnagill Moor. Here a distinct, initially grooved track slants up the right, and proves an effortless route onto the tops. *It affords a superb prospect over Roundhill Reservoir to the moorland bounding Upper Nidderdale, and also reveals Leighton Reservoir a long way back.*

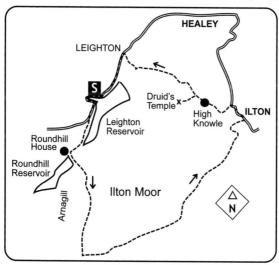

After an initial rise the way runs a largely level course parallel with the side valley of Arnagill down to the right. Characterful boulders are passed, including a huge individual block right by the path. The way reaches the modest outcrops of White Lodge Crags on the right just after crossing a stream. *This splendid vantage point demands an early break.* Resuming, the way runs on to join a broad track. *Visible in advance as it rolls down from the higher moor to the right, this inter-valley route dates from monastic times, connecting Upper Nidderdale with the Masham district. Packhorses would bring lead and wool from the Nidderdale estates for onward carriage to the abbeys at Fountains and Byland.*

Turn left in the foot and hoof steps of history. Over Sandy Hill (at 1168ft/356m the summit of the walk on Ilton Moor) the way rolls on. *Extensive views look across to Teesside, Roseberry Topping and the Cleveland and Hambleton Hills.* Gently declining through rampant heather, the track crosses a bridge and promptly forks at the site of High Langwith Cross.

While the right branch heads for Kirkby Malzeard, your left fork begins a more pronounced descent. Dropping through heather the moor is finally left at a gate above a plantation. Initially still a track, the way is soon overlaid by a surfaced farm road. At a junction at the end, forsake the road turning uphill in favour of the colourful walled track down to the left, with a view over to the tall spire of Healey church. On the edge of the scattered hamlet of Ilton its surface returns, passing a former Wesleyan Chapel of 1876.

At the junction by the open green, turn left down the road past the phone box, soon descending sharply to cross Sole Beck. A footbridge waits patiently for a deluge to flood the road. Within 50 yards leave by an enclosed track on the left, soon breaking free to run as a lovely green way outside the plantation. At a gate ignore the stile into the trees and turn up the far side of the wall. A grassy track climbs two fields to renovated High Knowle. Cross a fence-stile at the top and go left outside the buildings and yard, and through a gate join its drive. This rises away through a couple of fields to emerge onto Knowle Lane, the road to the Druid's Temple.

The walk returns to this point after a detour to the folly. Turn left up the road to a car park, and head through Druid's Plantation on a solid track or a green pathway, returning by the other when the temple's environs have been explored. *The Druid's Temple is a folly for which the eccentric British have long been famous. It was constructed in 1820 by William Danby of Swinton Hall, as a useful way of employing his men. Oval in shape, the inner depths lead to 'The Tomb'. The full complement of standing stones is based on the real thing at Stonehenge. Certainly it exudes quite an atmosphere, particularly if alone on a wild day. Numerous other stone edifices are also spread about the woods.*

Return down the access road and from a stile in the fence on the left, cross the field with a line of telegraph poles bound for a gap in the plantations. *Elaborate gateposts here suggest redundant stones from the temple. Healey and Fearby villages are seen across the valley side beyond. Low Knowle Farm is below in an attractive landscape, with plantations backed by high moorland.* Through the gate go left outside the plantation on a fine, embanked green way to a similar break halfway down. A track comes up from the farm, and once through, turn down the fieldside with the green track that drops down to a ladder-stile. *This superb grassy rake affords extensive views over the Leighton district to Colsterdale's distant moors, while Leighton Reservoir shimmers just ahead.*

From the stile head diagonally left across the field to a stile in a descending fence, in the far corner above a group of trees. *Note the old boundary dyke here.* Continue away, dropping to the edge of a steep wooded bank above Pott Beck. Here a green track forms, slanting right down through scattered woodland, and crossing a track it zigzags down to the beck. Amid delightful surrounds turn upstream to cross a stone-arched bridge. The track climbs a wall-side to run right to a gate into a field. Bear right to ascend the fenceside to a farm bridge above a barn, then cross the next field to a gate at the far top corner on the edge of Leighton. Through it turn immediately left (not as per map) to rise up a short green way to the entrance to Leighton Hall Farm, here gaining the road through the farming hamlet. Go left along the Masham-Lofthouse road, concluding alongside Leighton Reservoir.

Roundhill Reservoir from White Lodge Crags

RIVER BURN

START Masham   Grid ref. SE 225807

DISTANCE 7 miles (11km)

ORDNANCE SURVEY MAPS
1:50,000
Landranger 99 - Northallerton & Ripon
1:25,000
Explorer 298 - Nidderdale
Explorer 302 - Northallerton & Thirsk

ACCESS Start from the town centre. Car parking in the market place. Served by bus from Ripon, Bedale and Leyburn.

Easy rambling in the gentle valley of the River Burn, visiting a lovely village before a lengthy spell on delightful riverbanks

Masham - prounounced 'Massam' - is a splendid small town above the banks of the Ure. Centrepiece is a massive market square with characterful shops, cottages and the old Town Hall. At one corner stands the church of St Mary the Virgin, its impressive 15th century spire on a Norman base. Attractive 19th century almshouses are spread about, endowed by the Vernon Harcourt family. A modest walking trail links a set of sculptures known as the Masham Leaves. From 1875 Masham had its own station at the terminus of a 7$\frac{1}{2}$-mile branch line from Melmerby on the old line north of Ripon, though this fully closed in 1963. A popular and long-established steam rally is held on the edge of town each July, and a sheep fair in September. Market days are Wednesday and Saturday (its charter was granted in 1393), while local crafts include glass blowing and pottery. Facilities include a Post office, shops, bank, cafes, a chippy and of course several pubs.

Masham is a long-established brewing centre, and remarkably in an age of takeovers and closures it has actually doubled its breweries. Theakstons is a Dales institution: in the 1960s a little known yet iconic brewer of then disappearing traditional ales, the real ale revival of the 1970s brought it to the fore. Falling prey to larger brewers it became part of a massive national concern, but happily returned to family independence in 2003. In the former Lightfoot Brewery, neighbouring Black Sheep is aptly named, for a disenchanted member of the Theakston family broke away to start this enterprise in 1992, and is now a familiar sight on Dales bars. Both breweries have visitor centres and run guided tours.

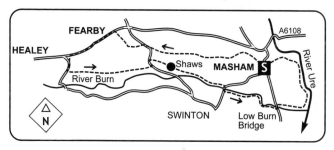

Leave the market place by Church Street, misleadingly at the opposite side to the church. At the bend at Park Square turn briefly right then left along a snicket. At the end this emerges onto Westholme Road alongside Theakston's Brewery. Turn right past the entrance and along the suburban street with a stream. At the sharp bend at the end go left over a stone-arched bridge, and along a lane past a large feeds mill. This ends as the mill does, continuing as a hugely inviting grassy cart track between hedgerows. Opening out into a field continue along the hedgeside, narrowing to a path beyond ramshackle barns to a gate at the end.

Through this turn sharp left over a trickle and along a grassy track to a gate, then bear slightly right across the field to a stile ahead. Bear right around the field, rejoining the grassy fieldside track to a corner gate. Though the track crosses the field centre, your way remains with the hedge on the right to a corner stile, swinging round the corner again and along to emerge onto a back road, Mickleby Lane. *To shorten the walk by a couple of miles (omitting Fearby), turn down the road for a minute to pick up the return route.* Turn right up the tarmac road, briefly, then take a stile on the left. Drop down the hedge as far as a stile in it, with another just yards further in another fence. Now cross to a stile opposite, and on again to one by a plank bridge. Rise to a corner gate just beyond, and a few steps further take a stile on the right. Up above are the houses of Fearby. Simply ascend the hedgeside to a wall-stile at the top, and cross a small enclosure to a gate onto the road through the village.

Turn left and take advantage of the capacious verges. *Fearby is a hugely attractive street village with a pub, the Black Swan, with its own camping/caravan site.* Keep straight on the length of the village, and at the top a footway (which serves the school) is a surprising bonus. *Big views look across the valley to mooorland sky-lines beyond.* Before the school, however, take a stile on the left and descend the field to one in another corner below, cutting the corner of a road junction. Descend the road for a couple of minutes just as far as the rough Low Moor Lane on the left. Turn along this for a pleasant, easy stride on an unerring course between hedgerows with good open valley views, eventually arriving back on Mickleby Lane. Turn left up it, briefly, then go right through a gate. A grassy track follows the hedgeside to a gate alongside a small plantation, just past which Shaws Farm appears (as does Masham's church spire).

Bear right towards it, encountering a stile before reaching the farm. Advance into the yard at the rear, but then bear left around the buildings on a fieldside to quickly join a track coming out from the farm. This runs pleasantly above a wooded bank dropping to the River Burn. When the track fades through a gate, bear right to drop down the declining bank to the very riverbank. Just beyond, a gate admits to the edge of Masham golf course. Simply forge straight on the side of the course, keeping faith with the river and ignoring any footbridges. Ultimately the path is deflected away by the clubhouse to cross to a gate onto a road alongside a sturdy stone-arched bridge. A seat tempts you to take a break.

Across the bridge, pass through a stile on the left to resume down the other bank of the river. The golf course remains, though beyond a stile a recommended riverside path keeps you off the course. The riverbank path is grand as you advance downstream, the Burn being good company as it leads to an eroded bend. Around it, the way drops down to cross a colourful pasture to a stile onto the road at Low Burn Bridge. _This is the well-named final bridge on the Burn._

Cross the bridge and turn right, resuming downstream on a delightful path between hedgerow and wooded bank, amid carpets of wild garlic. At the end the confluence with the Ure is unseen as a few steps take the path up to join the bank of the principal river. The conclusion is a delectable footpath upstream with the wide-flowing Ure, through lush surrounds. The church spire remains a permanent feature now, to draw you back to the square. This comes beyond a hedgerowed spell at the end, as the path is deflected from the river by the sewage works. An access track takes over to cross the Glebe, past Mill House and back up Millgate into a corner of the market place.

The River Burn at Low Burn Bridge

HACKFALL WOODS

START Grewelthorpe   Grid ref. SE 231761

DISTANCE 6^{1}2 miles (10^{1}2km)

ORDNANCE SURVEY MAPS
1:50,000
Landranger 99 - Northallerton & Ripon
1:25,000
Explorer 298 - Nidderdale

ACCESS Start from the village centre. Roadside parking. Served by very infrequent Ripon-Masham bus.

An extended ramble through beautiful woodland above the Ure

Grewelthorpe is a linear village featuring attractive cottages set back from spacious greens. St James church has a small bell turret, while a Methodist chapel stands redundant. A sloping green at the west end bears a crucifix and overlooks the Crown Inn, while towards the other end is a colourful pond. Leave the village by its eastern end, and a short way beyond the pond, as the road narrows to leave, take a gate on the left from where a splendid hedgerowed cart track heads away into rolling country. This soon drops down to swing right to a field, but take the gate in front and an even better green way runs a gem of an enclosed course. At the end ignore the gate in front, and take a stile on the right to resume along the holly hedgeside. From a stile at the end cross to a stile in the facing hedge, then bear left to one in the fence. *Massive views ahead look over the vale to the North York Moors.*

Head away to a stile opposite, and on again to the far end of the field, with a gate revealing Bush Farm in front. Cross to a stile in the hedge ahead, then bear right to the far corner of the field, keeping left of all farm buildings to drop to a gate in the corner. Entering a rougher slope, keep right with the fence as far as an old gateway, then drop down through a gate into the field below. Descend to the field bottom, then go left with the hedge outside the wood to a gate/stile in the corner, by a spring. Yards further take a gate/stile on the right into the woodland of Mickley Barrass.

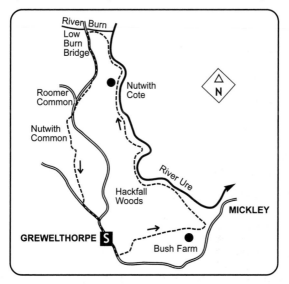

A good path heads away, running a level course to meet a broader path. Turn left to soon enjoy a splendid stride through the trees. Ignore a thinner branch rising left, and forge on through a bracken clearing, passing above a circular pool. Dropping down, cross a tiny stream to enter Hackfall Woods. *Acquired by the Woodland Trust in the 1980s, these were landscaped and filled with an assortment of 18th century follies and grottoes by William Aislabie of Studley Royal, and have only recently been restored: Victorian visitors paid to explore this fascinating setting.* There now follows a sustained mercurial section closer to the river, with steep banks above, and wild garlic carpets all around. After a stream crossing, with an island in the river alongside, three ways depart. Take the central one, inviting old stone steps climbing to a folly unexpectedly lurking just above. *A stone lintel carved 'WA 1730' is a reminder of Aislabie.*

Take the broad path continuing along a neck of land, at once joined by the earlier left branch. A little further is a fork, remain on the main, right branch. This leads to a staggered crossroads, with a branch doubling back left. Instead cross the stream in front, and another fork. *The left branch offers a two-minute detour as a super path rises to another folly, this of rougher hewn blocks alongside a stagnant pond.* Back at the fork the lower path runs grandly on, dropping through rampant wild garlic and absorbing the earlier lower path and around a big river bend. Just beyond, the public path is signed uncertainly left, as a much thinner path rising up the bank away from the broad riverside way: they soon re-unite. The upper path does a neat little zigzag featuring old stone steps, to quickly surmount the brow of Limehouse Hill. *This reveals a fine cameo ahead of the river backed by Masham's tall church spire.*

A little further the broader path rejoins, and you run on to a corner of the wood. While a path rises left, take the kissing-gate in front and head along a field bottom outside the trees. Further on, a kissing-gate re-admits to Nutwith Cote Wood, and a good path slants down through plantations to the riverbank. This now runs a super course upstream, rising at the end on a track to a gate out of the trees. Ignore the green track continuing up, and return to the steep wooded bank above the river, tracing this to drop just before the end to a stile below. Up above is Nutwith Cote Farm. Even more enjoyable walking takes over as you trace the grassy bank upstream. Further, the inflowing River Burn deflects the path away from the Ure. Tracing the soon to be revealed beck, a grassy way runs upstream to the road at Low Burn Bridge. *This is the well-named final bridge on the Burn (see page 57).*

Double back left along the road for a good half-mile to enter the open country of Roomer Common. At once bear left on a cart track rising away, running a super course up the common. *Looking back, Masham is dominated by its tall spire.* Higher, as you near the road, keep on a narrower way between wall and scrub, running a parallel course to the road to only rejoin it at the very end of the common. Here cross to the foot of the plantations of Nutwith Common. Follow the hard track just a few strides then bear left on a clear, more inviting footpath. This rises grandly through the trees to meet a forest road. Cross straight over to the left-hand path ascending stiffly to join a higher forest track. The continuation is unclear: go right fifty yards and a faint path rises left to quickly join an excellent path on the wood-top ridge. Go left on this a short way until a clear path branches right, dropping to a gate in a wall out of the trees. A slender trod slants left up the scrubby bank to a stile. *Pause here to look east over the vale to the Hambleton Hills fronting the North York Moors, with Whitestone Cliff prominent.*

Through the stile rise a short way with the hedge then take a stile in it. *Over to the left is an Ordnance Survey column at 705ft/215m on Horsepasture Hill, but more interesting is the well-defined bank of an ancient enclosure, highlighted by an old wall. Big views look south towards Kirkby Malzeard with the Dallowgill moors beyond, and the edge of Grewelthorpe in view just below.* A path slants diagonally down to a stile opposite. Continue the slant down the next field to another stile. The final field is crossed to the opposite corner, though if ploughed it is easier to keep left along the wallside, following the grassy headland past Hedgehog House and around to a stile onto a road. Go left along its verges to the edge of the village, bearing right at the sloping, triangular green by the old smithy to re-enter the main street.

*A Folly in
Hackfall
Woods*

WEST TANFIELD

START West Tanfield   Grid ref. SE 269788

DISTANCE 7 miles (11km)

ORDNANCE SURVEY MAPS
1:50,000
Landranger 99 - Northallerton & Ripon
1:25,000
Explorer 298 - Nidderdale

ACCESS Start from the village centre. Car park. Served by bus from Ripon and Masham.

> The River Ure leads out and back to this charming village, with two other attractive villages sandwiched in between

West Tanfield is most favourably viewed from its bridge on the Ure: dating from around 1734, this fine three-arched structure makes an impressive gateway into the village. St Nicholas' church dates back to the 14th century, though much restored in the 19th century. Among its tombs are splendid effigies of Sir John Marmion and his wife from around 1400. Alongside the church is the Marmion Tower, a 600-year old gatehouse to a long-disappeared manor house: spiral steps lead to the first floor to look over the village. Alongside the bridge is the Bull Inn, while at the cross-roads is the Bruce Arms with its old stables signage. Adjoining the Methodist Church of 1901 is its predecessor bearing a lintel of 1798. There is also a Post office/shop. This was the only station on the 7$\frac{1}{2}$-mile branch line to Masham, which finally closed in 1963.

Leave by crossing Tanfield Bridge. *Note the perilous stepped stile down the right side, though you needn't use it!* The main route sets off along a farm road on the right, running to within yards of Quarry House Farm (further than per map) before taking a stile on the left. An enclosed green track runs into a field behind the farm, from where cross diagonally to the river: in the corner is a kissing-gate into the foot of a wooded bank. An alternative start enjoys a riverbank spell, a permissive route courtesy of Tanfield Lodge Estate: across the bridge join the river (so you could use the airy stile!) and trace a path upstream around the wide sweep of Greensit Batts, finishing on a flood embankment to enter undergrowth at the rear of Quarry House Farm. The path runs to a stile into the field behind the farm, and beyond that the main route is joined just prior to entering the wood via a kissing-gate near the corner. In the corner just beyond is a stile into the trees.

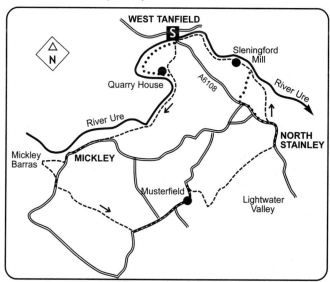

A good path scales the wooded bank then runs on the steep flank before dropping back down. The path runs grandly on to join the river for an excellent stride, and along to a fork on entering trees. To the left is Old Sleningford Farm. Take the left branch along the edge of the wood, over a stone slab on the stream and out into a field. Advance along the wood edge, and at the end a stile leads through a clear break in the wooded belt to emerge, revealing the edge of Mickley ahead. Bear left through park-like surrounds, a line of trees pointing to the nearest cottages, where a stile admits onto a short driveway onto the road at the eastern end of the village. Turn right along the street.

Mickley is a tiny but attractive street village, a riot of spring-time colour. The little church of St John has a bell-cote. At the far end the road climbs away alongside the start of the woodland of Mickley Barras. Part way up, before a steeper climb, a clear path delves into the trees. This runs on to an early fork. Ignore the broader path dropping right, and take that rising slightly left. This continues on closer to the wood top. After dropping to cross a small stream, the path rises to a junction. Here double back left on a thinner but still clear path, which runs a level course beneath the wood top to leave the trees at a gate/stile. Turn left a few steps to another gate/stile beneath a spring, and continue away along the fieldside, following the left-hand hedge all the way to a gate/stile onto a back road.

Turn right a short way, and at the foot of the slope escape left through a gate. A good cart track heads away to a gate into the small copse of Coal Bank Wood. Simply remain on this same bridle-path all the way along, soon emerging to run a delightful course through a part wooded valley alive with bluebells. Ultimately the path swings right at the end to a gate out of the trees. Advance along the hedgeside (beware of a moist moment) and on to a gate at the end, then swinging around to a gate onto a back road at Frizer Hill. Go left, enjoying a superb springtime daffodil display for half a mile, and ignoring junctions to left and right. *At the Ripon one, note an old boundary stone inscribed 'Musterfield 1837'.*

Passing Musterfield Farm, the path diverts to avoid a quarry. Advance to the bend after the farm, and a few strides further take a gateway in the hedge on the right. The bridleway doubles back right along the fieldside and down the wood edge to join a firm track at the bottom. Turn right on this, soon encountering the deep, working quarry on your right. Part way along the track swings sharp left, passing further old quarries alongside Fiveponds Wood before running more pleasantly on, and slowly down, with views to the North York Moors. The improving way drops steadily down until a sharp turn right. With North Stanley in view just ahead, pass through a gate in front to maintain the straight line, down a field-side to a kissing-gate at the end. Pass through the suburbia of Cock Pit Close onto the A6108 through North Stainley.

Cross the road and turn left along the verge. *North Stainley is a straggling main road village with attractive ponds on open greens. It boasts a Post office/shop, WC and two pubs, the Cross Keys and the Staveley Arms. just opposite the cricket pitch is the modest mid-19th century church of St Mary the Virgin with its bell-cote. Unseen on the southern edge of the village is the vast and popular theme park of Lightwater Valley.* Keep straight on out of the village. The true right of way leaves by the penultimate drive on the right just before the de-restriction sign, though at the time of writing it was closed due to erosion of the riverbank. On my visit an absence of notices meant I inadvertently undertook the full walk without hindrance, unaware of the closure - though care would certainly be needed if further erosion occurred.

Should things be re-instated, then follow the drive to the end cottage, where the path slips down to the right between gardens to a small gate, then on to a stile just ahead. *Nearby Sleningford Grange was once a grange of Fountains Abbey.* It then bears left along the fieldside, but just before the unseen river, slants left up a small bank to run along its top to suddenly overlook the river. The path then simply traces the bank top upstream, past the eroded section. Ultimately the path runs by scrub into trees and along to a better grassy way, where the replacement route comes in. The replacement involves tramping the A6108 verge further until reaching a gate on the right, from were a broad grassy path heads away. This runs a direct and very pleasant course to a kissing-gate at the far end, where the original line is rejoined. The river is currently absent, being hidden beyond the scrub of Mill Batts.

Turn left on the continuing grassy way, a caravan site is soon entered, and the path runs on to the cluster of reception buildings, including a small shop. To the right is the splendid old Sleningford Watermill in a lovely riverbank setting. *The river here flows wide and lively, and is popular with canoeists. Fee-paying picnickers are also welcome!* Follow the access road out, and a little beyond the gates, where it turns up towards the main road, take a path to the right to remain with the river. This traces the Ure upstream past a wide weir on a bend to return to the bridge at West Tanfield.

16

LAVER COUNTRY

START Kirkby Malzeard   Grid ref. SE 235743

DISTANCE 8 miles (13km)

ORDNANCE SURVEY MAPS
1:50,000
Landranger 99 - Northallerton & Ripon
1:25,000
Explorer 298 - Nidderdale

ACCESS Start from the village centre: the walk begins from the eastern end. Roadside parking. Occasional Ripon-Masham bus.

> A leisurely amble round villages above the River Laver, free of crowds, entirely rural, visiting interesting buildings and places

Kirkby Malzeard is a lengthy street village, one-time administrative centre of a vast area. A market charter was granted in 1307, and the replacement buttercross of 1868 occupies the main crossroads. A circular pinfold stands at one end of the village. Markets and fairs drew the monks of Fountains and Byland, who came by way of moorland roads from their Nidderdale estates. On a knoll in the wood behind the village stood the castle of Roger de Mowbray, son of Nigel de Albini who came over with the Conqueror: it was destroyed during a rebellion against Henry II. A 500-year old tower and a Norman doorway remain at St Andrew's church, much rebuilt after severe fire damage in 1908: the mouse symbol of Robert Thompson of Kilburn is in evidence in the Lady Chapel. The church is surrounded by some very old gravestones. A unique pub name celebrates the longevity of Henry Jenkins, born in 1500 and who supposedly lived an astonishing 169 years. There is a second pub, the Queens Head, a Post office, shop, tearoom and chip-shop.

Leave the cross by turning east along the Ripon road. *Set back on the left is the rather grand Mowbray House, beyond which is Wensleydale Creamery's Kirkby Malzeard dairy.* The road descends to Creets Bridge. *Note the proud gateposts on the left, with coats of arms, alongside attractive woodland.* Over the bridge, turn right along the drive towards Lawnwith Farm with the stream alongside. Leave however, at a kissing-gate on the left before entering the trees. From a stile at the end cross a field to a stile opposite, then rise away alongside a fence. Beyond an intervening stile keep on past the edge of a wood. From its corner a thin path crosses the centre of a crop field.

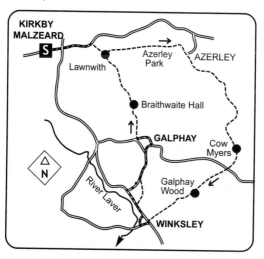

At the end sanity returns in the appealing sheep pastures of Azerley Park. Head directly away, and beyond an intervening stile a fence is followed towards the trees at Azerley. At the end bear right to a stile by a gate, entering a lawn with a house just ahead. Fork immediately right on a super green pathway through the woods in the company of Kex Beck. Ignore an early fork left and remain with the beck. Passing a pond it runs on through trees and past a cottage to the access road into Azerley: cross straight over and along the drive past Grange Farm to Home Farm. The track continues past it and runs on for a considerable time, often between hedgerows. Ignoring left turns to the folly of Azerley Tower and then Eight Acre Wood, the track swings right and drops appreciably. It ends at the bottom as two hedgerows head away. A waymark confirms you turn left alongside a sparse hedge towards the wood at the end. Swing right outside the trees and drop to a stile just below, then cross to a footbridge on Kex Beck.

In the field behind, cross to a clump of trees secreting the Witch-of-the-Woods House. *Though first impression is of a ruinous barn, a glimpse through the surround of trees sees a mysterious residence: on my 1993 visit stiles gave access, and a snatched glance through the window revealed a simply furnished room, complete with a table set for a meal. Today entry is restricted by a gate marked private.* On the other side rise right to a gate in the fence opposite. Through it a grassy track runs left along the other side, through more gates and along to Cow Myers Farm. Head between the buildings and out along its drive onto the Galphay-Ripon road above the River Laver.

Cross straight over and along the drive to Galphay Wood. The drive runs on through lovely park-like grounds high above the river. When the house appears just ahead, leave by a gate on the right and follow the opposite side of the hedge along past the house, to a corner gate. The edge of an unkempt enclosure leads to a second gate into a better field. Horse-riders are requested to stay on the (invisible) track, an informal diversion from the right of way. This runs left, through a gate and up the fieldside to another gate just short of Laver Banks Farm. The right of way ascends the hedgeside on your right, to step over a fence in a gap in the hedge at the top. Here turn left to a contrastingly splendid stile in a hedge, then rise right alongside the hedge. At the top corner pass through a small wooded bank at the top corner and along above the farm to join its drive at the end. Ahead is the bulky tower of Winksley church, and the drive leads down into the village.

Tiny Winksley overlooks the Laver and is dominated by the church of St Cuthbert & St Oswald, just along to the left. It dates from 1917, on the site of a chapel built by Abbot Marmaduke Huby of Fountains Abbey. For a tiny circuit, take the road down the near side of the churchyard to a crossroads, then turn right past the phone box and attractive cottages. *Countryman House on the right is the former Countryman Inn, a fairly recent casualty of modern times, when rural pubs far often offer greater value as residential property.* Rejoining the top road turn left to leave the village along the lane above Winksley Banks.

While the easy option is to remain on the road to a junction where turn right for Galphay, the map shows a short-cut path. On the ground this virtually abandoned route is currently less use than the map suggests. It begins by taking a gate on the right just before the road swings left into trees. Cross towards the field corner, but with no way through you must resort to a gate to the right. Bear left over the brow and down to the field corner, then right until halfway along. Negotiate an old fence and descend the right side of a hedge along to a gate onto West Lane just short of a barn. Go right into Galphay.

Galphay boasts a hugely attractive village centre with its many clusters of colourful cottages and gardens. Its large, sloping green sports a tall maypole restored in 1999, while a small stream tinkles through a smaller, lower green. A circular pinfold on your approach to the village was restored in 2002 by the Lord of the Manor, and its delightful garden makes the perfect spot for a refreshment break (as does the pub, of course!)

Winksley Church

69

Turn left at the green past the Galphay Inn to a sharp bend, where impressive gates front the drive to Braithwaite Hall. This direct way to the hall has an alternative which goes briefly left on the road, there taking a kissing-gate on the right at a junction. An invisible path runs on through the park grounds, parallel with the drive but pleasanter. Beyond a miry pond it swings right to rejoin the drive at a cattle-grid to enter the inner grounds, with farm buildings to the left. Take the main drive ahead, curving left down to the front of the hall. *Architecturally very characterful, its great roof appears to entirely overburden the stone walls beneath. On the right is a large duckpond.*

Immediately in front turn sharp right, as the drive heading away transforms into a green way. At the end take the right-hand gate to enter a large sheep pasture. Keep near the left-hand fence to descend to a corner gate. Through it, an access track is joined to lead back over Kex Beck to Lawnwith and its drive onto the road at Creets Bridge. Return up the road, noting, immediately after the dairy, a dark snicket offers a conclusion by way of the churchyard.

Kirkby Malzeard

17

COLSTERDALE

START Gollinglith Foot   Grid ref. SE 153809

DISTANCE 5³4 miles (9km)

ORDNANCE SURVEY MAPS
1:50,000
Landranger 99 - Northallerton & Ripon
1:25,000
Explorer OL30 - Yorkshire Dales North/Central
Explorer 302 - Northallerton & Thirsk

ACCESS Start from a parking area by the phone box. Reached from a side road off the Masham-Lofthouse road a good half-mile west of Healey (signed 'Colsterdale'). • OPEN ACCESS - see page 8.

> *A delectable ramble penetrating the unfrequented upper valley of the River Burn by way of a classic green road*

Unless the River Burn is very low, eschew the ford in favour of a footbridge from the corner of the parking area. From it turn upstream, past an attractively located cottage to rejoin the road from the ford: this at once becomes a track, on through a gate to run past a farm. Ignore the turn into the farm, and as the old road swings left just beyond, advance through a gate in front to begin a long march along the Coal Road. *The Coal Road runs a magnificent route along the south side of Colsterdale, a gem of an old way largely untarnished by modern-day use: truly a classic.*

Colsterdale was exploited for coal by the monks of Jervaulx Abbey, having been granted mining rights by the influential land-owners the Scropes in 1334, and was still being mined until much more recent times. The Coal Road lives up to its name by providing access to long defunct pits in the upper reaches of the River Burn.

Glorious panoramas reveal much of the Colsterdale scene. During these early stages enjoy the especially rich colour of Birk Gill Wood in the side valley opposite. Above, and more prominent, are Slipstone Crags fronting Agra Moor and the bracken-clad moorland of Long Side. Looking enviably resplendent are scattered farms and cottages amid the fields immediately across your own valley.

The track levels out at a prominent, grassed-over pit, every aspect becoming more exquisite as the immediate surrounds turn as colourful as the valley scenes. Through the next gate heather takes over alongside a line of gnarled hawthorn, and the entire scene takes on a wilder mantle as the dalehead appears. At the next gate open country is entered and the now more standard track forges on. Eventually the first farm in the valley, aptly named High House (formerly Colsterdale House), appears on the opposite bank. The track drops towards it, where a stone bridge arches the Burn. *For a shorter circuit, cross the bridge to the farm and return along the road.*

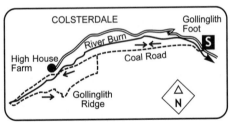

Resuming upstream, regain the main track, passing through a gate warning of old mine workings. At this point take a grassy path bearing right onto the bank and cross, in normal conditions by a single stride at a narrow rocky passage. *The grassy sward here is a lovely spot to linger by the sparkling Burn.* Resume by following a thin trod upstream. *Remember too that entering old workings can be dangerous!* Passing various sites of small workings, the stream leads along to join a shooters' track at a bridge. Turn left over it, with the confluence of the Burn and Thorny Grane Gill just to the left. Just up the slope is a junction beneath a suburban looking shooters' house dated 1898. *Near here in 1709 colliers cut through veins of lead, and though exploited, the modest amounts never approached the value of the coal deposits.*

Turn left here, at once bridging the colourful sidestream of Thorny Grane Gill and doubling back down the valley on this good track which you left earlier. Although you could simply remain on it back to the bridge at High House, within a few minutes comes a more adventurous alternative as a shooters' track slants up to the right before levelling out. *This splendid promenade affords grand views across the valley, down to Slipstone Crags beyond the green pastures.* At a circular shooting butt it swings uphill, revealing the Twin Standing Stones on the skyline just above. Levelling out on Gollinglith Ridge alongside another butt, leave it and cross to the Twin Standing Stones.

Perched on a boulder, this landmark pair of cairns' name is somewhat baffling, they being neither twins nor standing stones. Resume along the vague edge, scattered rocks leading to a sizeable cairn above the principal outcrops of Gollinglith Crags. *Piles of stones below are the remains of abandoned quarry workings.* Decline gently along to a wall ahead, then descend alongside it on a super green path, rather steeply at the bottom to land you back on the Coal Road. Turn right to conclude the walk as you began on this luxuriant trail.

The Twin Standing Stones, Gollinglith Crags

73

SLIPSTONE CRAGS

START *Gollinglith Foot*   *Grid ref. SE 153809*

DISTANCE *7 miles (11km)*

ORDNANCE SURVEY MAPS
1:50,000
Landranger 99 - Northallerton & Ripon
1:25,000
Explorer OL30 - Yorkshire Dales North/Central
Explorer 302 - Northallerton & Thirsk

ACCESS *Start from a parking area by the phone box. This is reached from the Masham-Lofthouse road a good half-mile west of Healey: the mile-and-a-bit-long dead-end road is signed 'Colsterdale'.* • *OPEN ACCESS - see page 8.*

A classic ramble over glorious moorland, with far-reaching views over lower Wensleydale and the closer delights of Colsterdale

From the parking area return just a few strides along the road and turn up a drive on the left before houses. This runs into a field before climbing steeply towards Agra Crags Plantation. Don't enter, but remain on the access road running left towards the farm at Low Agra. Before it, however, turn up outside the wall enclosing the plantation, ascending a colourful pasture of gorse, rocks and silver birch, with a part sunken old way. *Enjoy grand views over the farm, with the upper dale driving into the moors.* Higher up, a clearer track forms, crossing one linking the plantations either side, and continuing up to a gate in a wall at the top. A fainter grass track continues up the field past some rocks to the top corner of the plantation on the left. Levelling out, it runs on to a gate to become enclosed alongside a higher, smaller plantation at High Agra.

Advance along here until just short of the end (not as per map), where take a gate into the field on the left and follow the track around the fieldside to a gate near the far end. An extensive rolling moorland is now spread ahead. The track crosses a field centre, through a fence-gate and temporarily fades as you cross the next pasture to drop left to cross a tiny stream, then rising by an old sunken way to a wall-gate. Again fading, head directly away across the field centre, the high point of this stage. Tranmire farm stands over to the left, a cosy arrangement under its shelter-belt of trees. Through a gate at the end you enter open access moorland. Though the track heads off right, your grassy path is straight ahead, descending pleasantly through bracken into the heather. *As you drop down, note the Tranmire Stone set into the sturdy wall junction to your left: this boundary stone is inscribed with a hand and 'East Witton' and 'Mashamshire'.*

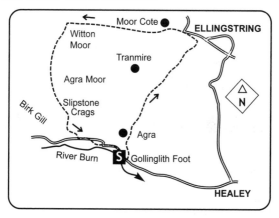

The thin path simply runs along the wallside, over a stream and a small marsh. Passing another boundary stone the way is sent over a ladder-stile (not as per map) to resume on the other side of the wall, through a small gate and on to a plantation corner. Simply forge on the excellent wallside path along this delectable, colourful moor. *At least three further identical boundary stones are set into the wall. Over the brow the views north open out to reveal lower Wensleydale, with Thornton Steward village straight ahead.*

As you drop down towards the end of the moor, fields appear ahead. *An option is to keep on to a gate off the moor and descend the field to the road at Keepers Cottage on the edge of Ellingstring, then go left along the road: at a sharp bend, advance straight on through the gate and along the continuing access road.* The best route remains on the moor by dropping left into a green basin surrounded by bracken: cross to the low brow on its other side, and bear left to pick up an improving track on it. This runs on, slanting down towards the road below, but remaining on the moor to meet an access road at the moor corner.

Head left along the rough access road, ignoring its branch to the farm at Moor Cote and remaining on the moor edge to rise to a gate in a wall. Through this it forks: the left branch goes to Tranmire, but your way is the right one, striding grandly over Witton Moor alongside a plantation. Levelling out, tracks go out to and return from a shooters' cabin on Tranmire Hill. *Ahead is the distinctive profile of Great Roova Crags across the expanse of Caldbergh Moor, and then as the plantation ends, things open out to reveal a bigger sweep of your own Witton Moor, with Great Haw and South Haw beyond Colsterdale Moor, and the Leyburn area over to the right through the dip past Witton Fell and the Sowden Beck valley. All this is very, very good.*

Soon after a gentle drop, a crossroads is reached with the East Witton-Colsterdale track coming through the gate on the right. This crossroads marks the start of the triangle's third side. Turn left on the rough way rising gently across the open moor. Abuse by trail bikers has left it untidy until levelling out on the top, a dead-flat section where the watershed crossing onto Agra Moor is marked by a solitary boundary stone to the left and a minor ditch to the right. *At around 1082ft/330m this is the high point of the walk.* Finest feature is the fact that the track at once transforms into a good, firm way, and remains so as it begins a steady decline back into Colsterdale.

As the track becomes stonier Slipstone Crags appear ahead amid glorious mixed scenery as the moor drops away. *The birch-lined stream of Brown Beck tumbles into the woods of Birk Gill at the bottom, with Colsterdale's green pastures on the tongue ahead, and the Burn valley beyond.* Although you can simply remain on this path as it curves down beneath the gritstone edge, better to take a closer look: at a path-side stone before the start of the rocks, a trod turns up to the left, then turns to run along to the crest of the true start. The top of the outcrops can be followed all the way along. *A climbers' path runs along their base.*

Slipstone Crags is a rock climbers' dream, easy of access and in a beautiful, south-west facing setting. It has yielded scores of routes along the length of its clean buttresses, many surprisingly relatively lately developed. As the rocks fade out, West Agra Plantation is just ahead. A path slants down from the last boulders, through bracken to the wall beside which it descends pleasantly to rejoin the main path as it passes through a gate in the wall. Just yards further take the right branch of this green way, slanting down through bracken to a gate onto the little Colsterdale road.

Turn left for 150 yards, where a thin path slants right through bracken to a stile in a gateway in the descending wall. Pass to the right of the garden at Body Close and join the grassy drive at the other side, running out to rejoin the road at the foot of a hairpin bend. Resume along the road, this final half-mile being a traffic-free delight in the company of the River Burn.

Slipstone Crags

BRAITHWAITE MOOR

START East Witton   Grid ref. SE 144860

DISTANCE 8¼ miles (13km)

ORDNANCE SURVEY MAPS
1:50,000
Landranger 99 - Northallerton & Ripon
1:25,000
Explorer OL30 - Yorkshire Dales North/Central
Explorer 302 - Northallerton & Thirsk

ACCESS Start from the village centre. Roadside parking. Served by bus from Leyburn and Masham. • OPEN ACCESS - see page 8.

An invigorating tramp across the moors with magnificent views over Wensleydale, and history too - save this for a clear day

East Witton suffered terribly in the plague of 1563, and was rebuilt as an estate village by the Earl of Ailesbury at the start of the 19th century. The church of St John the Evangelist, built in 1809, stands just east of the village. Two lines of houses are set back from a vast, sweeping green, which features a quoits pitch and an old water pump. High up the green is an old Methodist chapel of 1882, and also a little Post office. At the main crossroads stands the Blue Lion pub, as well as an attractive former school and a working tap embedded in a boulder.

From the crossroads adjacent to the main road at the east end of the village, turn south along the cul-de-sac Lowthorpe past the Parish Room of 1929. At the first bend, alongside attractive three-storey Lowthorpe Farm, turn right along a rough road, Sowden Beck Road. This immediately commences a steep climb, a sustained pull that deals with the climbing within the first half-hour. *Savour big views back over village and valley, and out across the Vale of Mowbray to the long skyline of the North York Moors.* Though the surface alternates, the same road remains underfoot as the going eases alongside plantations under Witton Fell. Levelling out on the high point, your impending moors are revealed just ahead. The track turns left through a gate at the end, revealing its objective of Sowden Beck Farm in the dip below. The access road drops to a ford and footbridge on Sowden Beck to reach the isolated farm.

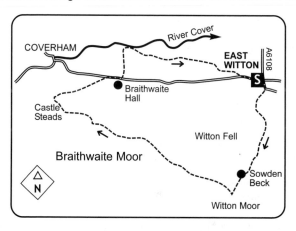

Pass the front of the house to a gate behind, then rise up the right-hand wallside, a track forming towards the end to reach a gate onto Witton Moor. Faced with a crossroads of ways, turn right along the shooters' track. As the wall quickly turns away, remain on the track heading directly across the moor. It drops to ford Tom Claypham Beck then ascends past a lone tree and on to ford the smaller Sowden Beck. *On the other bank are the scant remains of old coal workings, the first of several over the next mile or so.* Up the other side, ignore a branch right and remain on the track straight ahead across the heathery expanses of Braithwaite Moor. *A little further, the gentlest of brows sees moorland surrounds joined by a splendid wider prospect, across Wensleydale to Castle Bolton beneath the high moors dividing the valley from Swaledale.* This runs on to approach a boundary fence alongside a circular pit and ruin. *The view now also embraces the impressive Penhill End straight ahead.* Here the track doubles sharply back to the right. Ignore this and advance to a gate in the fence in front.

With no path now, go left a short way with the fence, then head directly away on a level course with an intermittent, reedy path through heather and a line of timber butts, with a steeper bank to your left. *Ahead is Middleham Low Moor, and to your right Middleham Castle itself.* A more obvious way soon forms, still not entirely clear: key is the line of old workings along this contour. The way remains flat and becomes surer as it passes above the next pit. Simply forge on, beneath another and on above one. A moister section precedes arrival at the last pit. With no further evidence of the path, bear right on one of the sheeptrods to join the parallel wall. Advance on trods through the bracken to the wall corner ahead. *A glimpse down Braithwaite Banks through the gateway just prior to the corner reveals Braithwaite Hall. This corner also marks the high point of the walk, a very modest 1150ft/350m, considering the amount of time spent on the moors.*

From the corner slant down the steeper slope and cross to a gate in the facing fence, just yards down from a lower wall corner that it strikes off from. Through the gate a path forms in bracken, heading away through an intriguing trough beneath the shapely ridge of Crundell Hill. Opening out, Penhill returns ahead, and the improved green way drops down at the end through a grassy basin, joining the wall alongside a small wooden gate built into it. This is the key to leaving the moor. Pass through and slant left with the wall, at the bottom corner dropping onto the grass platform of Castle Steads. *With grassy banks and ditch, this is the site of an Iron Age fort of the Brigantes. At this turning point of the walk you are overlooking the lower reaches of the side valley of Coverdale.*

Leave by slanting down again to the wall along the bottom. Turning right, the gate at the end takes you out of access land. Head away to one in a fence opposite, then advance on above a stand of trees, forging straight on the extensive Hanghow Pastures to ultimately slant down to a gate at the far corner. Joining a back road, resume on this to farm buildings at Cherry Hill. Braithwaite Hall is now well seen up to the right. *This impressive triple-gabled house dates from 1667, and is in the care of the National Trust. Still in use as a farm, it can be visited by prior arrangement.*

Opposite its drive take a gate on the left, and a cart track heads away through two fields to drop to Hullo Bridge on the River Cover. *Its stone arch sits amid splendid scenery as the Cover runs through a modest ravine and over a slabby limestone bed.* Don't cross but head downstream, quickly slanting to the bank top where the path runs on with a fence. At the end take a stile in it and advance the few yards to a wall-stile ahead. Now bear gently right across this large field, finding a small footbridge in a corner on the tree-lined stream. Head away with a fence, and through a gap in it to resume on the other side, along the tapering field to a gate at the end. A track takes over, but when it swings sharp right to East Witton Lodge, instead take a gate on the left and resume.

A path along the fieldsides leads past a clump of trees, and from a stile turn right along the edge, quickly left again to pass, enclosed, alongside the belt of trees. Shortly reaching a gate at the end, turn right on the cart track of West Field Lane which becomes enclosed to run a splendid hedgerowed course. When it turns sharp right to join a road, take a stile in front and along the fieldside to a wall-stile. East Witton re-appears ahead. Advance to a stile just to the right of a little barn, and remain on the hedgeside all the way to the end, with a gate onto the back road. The village is just a minute further, re-entering to tramp its lengthy sloping green.

*The Blue Lion,
East Witton*

20

JERVAULX ABBEY

START East Witton   Grid ref. SE 144860

DISTANCE 7$\frac{1}{2}$ miles (12km)

ORDNANCE SURVEY MAPS
1:50,000
Landranger 99 - Northallerton & Ripon
1:25,000
Explorer 302 - Northallerton & Thirsk

ACCESS Start from the village centre. Roadside parking. Served by bus from Leyburn and Masham.

A splendid walk combines a ruined abbey in a beautiful setting, a lovely old village and a delectable stretch of the River Ure

For a note on East Witton see page 78. From the crossroads adjacent to the main road at the east end of the village, head out on the Ripon road, past the pub to the church. The churchyard saves a little roadwork, just beyond which take a stile on the right. Cross a small stream and head directly away along the fieldside, crossing another stream and tumbledown stile to reach a stile at the end. Joining an access road, turn left (past a burial ground) and straight on through Waterloo farm. Running to bridge a stream the road then climbs to end at Thirsting Castle Lodge.

Go straight on over the bridge on the lively Deep Gill Beck, then the continuing track climbs steeply away, through a gate and up the field. *This affords big views over to Leyburn under a moorland skyline, with Danby Hall lower down the valley.* Ultimately the track reaches a wood on the far side to run to a corner. While the track passes through a gate to continue, don't follow it but turn left through the break in the trees to reveal Hammer Farm in front.

Pass through the gate and round to the right of the farm buildings, joining its driveway by the house at the front. Now simply follow its level driveway out along a defined shelf. *Long views look over the lower valley to the western scarp of the North York Moors, with Black Hambleton crowning the Hambleton Hills.*

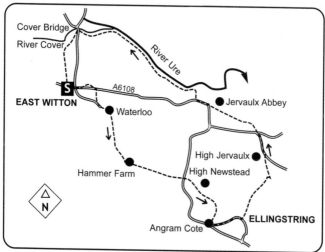

Cross over the road but ignore the drive to High Newstead Farm, instead take a stile on the right and cross the field to a gate in the top corner. Maintain the slant to a small gate in the fence ahead (not quite as per map), looking down on the farm. Again slant up to a stile in the top corner, this time accessing a surfaced access road to which the map makes no reference. Cross to a stile opposite and slant up the field, rising up the hedgeside to a gate at the top. Now advance along the enclosure to Angram Cote Farm just ahead, passing straight through to rise onto a road. *In front is an arch-headed well.* Turn left a few strides and then double back left down the road into Ellingstring, passing a triangular green.

Ellingstring is a lovely little village, well off the beaten track and sheltering beneath the edge of extensive moorland. Alongside a surprisingly extensive sloping green with its seats and daffodils, the old school still has its bell. A plain little Wesleyan Methodist chapel of 1848 stands boarded up. In the dip at the bottom is a Victorian postbox just before the phone box. Beyond is homely Lilac Cottage, for decades an old fashioned youth hostel until recent closure. Turn left along an enclosed driveway on the left to Ruskill Bank Farm, just before the postbox. Forking in front of the buildings, take the left branch which runs a pleasant hedgerowed course, dropping down to terminate with a bewildering choice of gates. Take the one on the left, yards before the track's demise.

Head away, but within a few strides bear right to a bridle-gate. Continue diagonally away from this, on through a gap in a hedge before it starts a steeper drop. Maintain the slant, dropping down by the forlorn remains of a hedge, with a sunken way, to a fence corner below. Continue along the fence to a bridle-gate at the very end. Don't pass through, but drop left to a ladder-stile over the wall in the corner. Head away with a tall hedge to a stile at the end, joining the A6108 alongside the drive to High Jervaulx Farm. *This is the home of the celebrated Brymor ice cream, and its attraction of ice cream parlour and coffee shop is a real tempter!*

Now follow the road, with care, briefly further left to drop to a junction with a side road. Escape through a gate in front alongside a lodge, into the tranquility of Jervaulx Park. An inviting grass track heads away to join a firmer carriageway ahead. The actual right of way bears left of the grass track, keeping a little higher as it runs on to a fence corner, on alongside trees and past a couple of houses before dropping gently to meet the carriageway much further along, with super views of the abbey.

Jervaulx Abbey is one of relatively few in private hands: admission is by means of a honesty box. Jervaulx was founded by Cistercian monks in 1156, having originated from Byland Abbey, and briefly set up near Aysgarth a decade earlier. The name is derived from Yore Vale, Yore being the old name for the River Ure. At the Dissolution in 1536, Jervaulx suffered particularly badly, and much of the stone was carted off for other buildings. The remains are less 'uniform' than those under official ownership, parts being positively draped in flowers.

The carriageway crosses over the abbey visitors' footpath, and in front of Jervaulx Hall, swings left out onto the A6108 again. Turn right for a few minutes only, this time with a sound path. After bridging a beck, pass through a gate on the right and a fieldside track takes you directly to the bank of the River Ure. Turn left upstream, commencing a mercurial stroll clinging close to the lush green bank. *The prow of Penhill End immediately appears up-dale, with Danby Hall seen across the river.* An old fishpond is passed and the super path runs on, noting the former Danby Low Mill on the opposite bank. A little further the confluence of Ure and Cover is met, and the latter river leads the final stage upstream to Cover Bridge. *Across this fine arched bridge stands the welcoming Cover Bridge Inn, another temptation difficult to ignore.*

The route however simply crosses the road, not the bridge, with spiral steps back down onto the bank. The first pasture is crossed centrally to a gate/stile part way along, then along a field-side to the next gate/stile. Here the wooded river swings off to the right, the path forks and your route sets off back to East Witton by crossing the field centre to a gate. Advance to a stile alongside the barn, then around the back to a wall-stile. Now simply head away on a straight line along several fieldsides, crossing a couple of watercourses en route and ascending to a brow. Just beyond a gate at the end, with the village outspread, a hedge gives way to a wall. Take a small gate in it and cross one last enclosure, emerging onto the village street alongside the old Methodist chapel.

Jervaulx Abbey

21

CONSTABLE BURTON

START *Thornton Steward   Grid ref. SE 181877*

DISTANCE *6¹4 miles (10km)*

ORDNANCE SURVEY MAPS
1:50,000
Landranger 99 - Northallerton & Ripon
1:25,000
Explorer 302 - Northallerton & Thirsk

ACCESS *Start from the Yorkshire Water car park at Thornton Steward Reservoir, north of the village.*

> *Two pleasant villages are linked by a charming beck*

Thornton Steward Reservoir was completed as recently as 1976, and holds some 218,000,000 gallons. Set in a curious upland bowl, it is used by both fishing and sailing clubs. Enter the confines of the reservoir and head left past the sailing clubhouse and boats. At the end turn right before the hedge, rising on a broad grassy way up the distinct bank. Keep rising past gorse bushes to the high point just ahead. *The reservoir now forms a foreground to the distant skyline of the Cleveland Hills and Hambleton Hills across the Vale of Mowbray. Of shapelier appeal is the profile of Penhill, to your left overlooking Wensleydale, with Braithwaite Moor to its left.*

Advance on, dropping to a dip and then up towards the tree-crowned knoll ahead. To its left a bridle-gate takes you out of the reservoir environs. Head away along a fieldside, descending to a stone bridge over a small stream at the bottom. The path runs on through colourful undergrowth, becoming enclosed to emerge at a modern house and farm. Its short drive leads out onto No Man's Moor Lane. Cross straight over and shadow telegraph poles across a ploughed field, soon joining a firm track. *If this is unappealing, you might go briefly right along the road to pick up the track from the start.* This leads over a gentle brow to reveal Finghall just ahead, and later becomes concreted to drop down onto Blew House Lane on the village edge. Go left to the central junction.

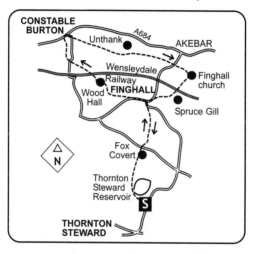

In front is the welcoming Queens Head. If you opt for a break here, remember there'll be a second chance when the walk returns to this point! Finghall is a tiny but attractive street village set on an elevated ridge. Just short of the junction stands an absolutely tiny former Wesleyan Chapel, while just beyond is the present red-brick chapel, built in 1909 by the Wesleyans. Finghall had its own station on the Northallerton & Hawes Branch of the North Eastern Railway, and the station buildings survive down the lane. The track survived into the 1990s thanks to military use, and after a massive effort by its supporters, re-opened as the Wensleydale Railway in 2003. So, Finghall's station exists again, currently the sole village station on the line's 17 miles from Leeming Bar to Redmire, the market towns of Bedale and Leyburn providing the other stations. Perhaps one day the line will resume its old course up the length of Wensleydale to meet the Settle-Carlisle line at Garsdale Head.

Turn left on the road out of the village, and as the road swings left keep straight on through a gate in front. Maintain this line along the fieldside, at the corner passing through to the other side. Entering a large sloping field bear left and down the side until level with the barns of Wood Hall. Go left along into the barnyard, and turn right behind an old barn at the end, down another cart track.

Approaching the farmhouse below, don't swing right to it but take a thin path into adjacent Croft Wood. Initially unclear, it drops steadily down through the odd fallen tree, its old green way quite distinct, initially. Then the path turns left and runs a level course through the wood, but within 150 yards take a less obvious faint branch right. This drops down to the railway line just below. Cross to find a splendid cart track curving left back into trees, declining gently to the far bottom corner of the wood. A couple of gates send the track across a field to join a road. *This was Constable Burton's link with its railway station up to the left.*

Go left 30 yards to find a stile in the wall on the right, to join a right of way descending the field. Bear right to a tiny footbridge in the facing hedge, then turn right along the hedge, crossing a footbridge on Sun Beck. Remain with the hedge on your right, through a gate and over a slight brow to a kissing-gate overlooking Constable Burton. Bear slightly left down the field to a gate onto the A684. *Constable Burton is a tiny village on the south side of the main road, while to the north stands Constable Burton Hall. Built in 1768 by renowned architect John Carr, it remains home to the Wyvills, one of the oldest families in the county. The hall is known for its beautiful gardens, open mid March to mid October. Focal point of the village is a sloping green between cottages and the beck, while its pub, the Wyvill Arms, is along the road west.* Yards to the right, turn along a side road above the green. *On your right is the old reading room and former school, still with its bell.* Swinging round the corner quickly turn left on Mill Lane, losing its surface at a former chapel. *To the left is the imposing Mill House.*

Continue along the cart track which runs a splendid course above wooded Burton Beck. At a fork keep straight on the lower option, through a gate/stile. Beyond the tiny sewage works comes the finest section of the walk, a delectable stroll on a slender green pasture with the beck alongside. A young plantation deflects briefly from the beck before a bridge leads out into a field. Keep left along the wooded edge. Though not as per map, a waymarked gate part way on puts you back into a beckside pasture. Continue - with Unthank Farm up the other bank - over a stile and at the end take a corner gate on the right back into the end of the ploughed field from earlier. Immediately use a gate on the left and a grassy track forms across this field, through a gate and on again to a stile at the far end. This gives a short spell in beckside trees - by now it is named Leeming Beck. Quickly taking a hurdle back into a field, cross to Leeming Beck Bridge at the end, with Finghall church seen beyond it. The road is joined at a gate to the right of the bridge.

Cross straight over and along the church drive. *With its central double bell-cote, the little church of St Andrew stands in curious isolation.* From a gate at the top corner of the churchyard, ascend pleasantly by a tiny stream. Entering a wooded gill slant up to a kissing-gate at the top, and resume on a faint path outside the gill. This section is not as per map. A gentle rise leads to re-crossing the railway line. Rise again up a field and cross to the top corner, where a kissing-gate sends you briefly right to another onto Spruce Gill Farm drive. Turn right along this surfaced lane which runs on to re-enter Finghall. Advance to the pub and return as you came.

The old mill, Constable Burton

89

SNAPE PARK & WELL

START Snape   Grid ref. SE 265843

DISTANCE $6^3$4 (or $5^3$4) miles (11km)

ORDNANCE SURVEY MAPS
1:50,000
Landranger 99 - Northallerton & Ripon
1:25,000
Explorer 302 - Northallerton & Thirsk

ACCESS Start from the village centre. Roadside parking. Served by bus from Masham and Bedale.

> Two historic villages are linked by open fields, broken up by neat woodland paths

Snape is a splendid little street village, best known for its castle, stood in isolation at the western end. Built as a manor house in the first half of the 15th century, the great hall and chapel are the best surviving features. Catherine Parr, later wife of Henry VIII, lived here while married to John Neville. The great house underwent periods of neglect until acquired by William Milbank of nearby Thorpe Perrow in 1798. Though in private hands the castle is well seen from the road and the chapel approach. An integral part of the main building, the impressive St Mary's chapel still serves the parish of Well with Snape, and can be visited by a path along the edge of the adjacent yard. Focal point of village life is the Castle Arms. The game of quoits is played here, one of numerous local activities to feature on the Millennium Stone on the village green. The green extends a considerable length of the village and a stream runs through: two village pumps still stand, as does a memorial to Lady Augusta Milbank who died in 1874.

Head east along the main street and out on the Carthorpe road. The houses end at once, and a couple of minutes further a stile is reached on the right. *Note the benchmark on the old gatepost.* Head away along the hedgeside, to the far end where a footbridge puts you in the next field. Advance to the end and bear left along the top side. *Big views look left to the Hambleton Hills and, further north, the Cleveland Hills.* Reaching a corner, turn through the large gap and resume with the hedge on your left. Towards the end advance to a stile in the corner.

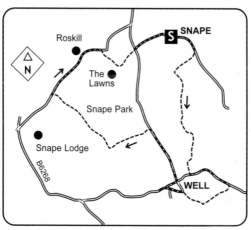

With a tall hedge to your left, head away along a delightful sheep pasture which slowly tapers to a stile at the end. *Here a large hare and I shared the surprise as it sprang from beneath my feet to bound away.* Now follow the right edge of a field a short way, then pass through a gap on a farm bridge on Low Park Beck. On the other side bear left into a wooded corner (perhaps seeing a waymark on a tree), where a clear path suddenly forms to run left through the belt of woodland. Bear right at an early fork to soon emerge into another large field. Well awaits, just ahead now.

Advance to the corner just ahead, noting a reedy pond to your left. Crossing a farm track the official line is straight across the field centre, keeping right of a line of telegraph poles and aiming left of the church. If the field is ploughed it may be easier to go left a little to afford a more pleasant crossing. At the far side turn right along the hedge as far as a telegraph pole. Now the path turns left for the village, leaving the field to become enclosed alongside a dry channel. It then swings right and along to a fork in front of a local brewery depot. Opt for the kissing-gate on the left to run by the churchyard and out onto Church Street in Well.

Saving a mile, the direct route turns right to the staggered crossroads by the pub. For an interesting loop, turn left on this minor road leaving the village, soon passing the old school. Keep on a few minutes until a gentle bend left, where take a gate on the right. Head away along two short fieldsides (swapping midway) to a gate into a large field. Bear right around the edge to a footbridge at the end. Head away along the hedgeside to a corner stile, then ascend the short hedgeside to the start of a grassy track. *To the south-east is a large lake at the Nosterfield quarry.* Follow this throughout its course, initially sunken and later enclosed to emerge onto a sharp bend of the road through Well.

Turn left, ascending Well Bank to reach a seat at the top. *This is an essential halt to enjoy a super view over the rooftops of Well and across the flat but colourful Vale of Mowbray to the long line of the Cleveland and Hambleton Hills.* Resuming, turn down the side road through trees to a junction in front of a lodge and pond. While your route is right, first go left 150 yards to find a stile in the low wall on your right. Immediately at your feet is St Michael's Well. *Here clear water appears and runs into the beck. A stile on the other side accesses a low cliff from where water originally flowed.* Back on the road you enter the village centre. *Well is an attractive village sheltering beneath its steep bank. Focal point is the junction where the Milbank Arms stands. Along the side street are the Hall and some old almshouses. The church of St Michael is a lovely old place featuring some Neville tombs. Note also the exceptionally tall old cross shaft at the front of the churchyard. Evidence of a Roman bath house has also been discovered here.*

Leave by heading along the Snape road, which is followed out of the village for around ten minutes. Reaching a distinctive belt of trees, turn up its near side on a good fieldside track. At the field top this turns into the trees. Don't re-emerge at the other side, but turn unconvincingly up the centre of the wood, known as The Belt. Almost at once a good little path forms, ascending unfailingly for some time until swinging right to a gateway. From a stile cross to the corner of Grays Plantation ahead. *The drop of the slope of the old deer park of Snape Park beneath you affords better views over the Vale of Mowbray, with the celebrated landmark of Roseberry Topping discerned at the northern limit of the Cleveland Hills.*

A little path runs along the wood top. Emerging, descend to a stile by a pond to join a drive. Just to the right take a stile to ascend a hedgeside with an isolated house to the left. From a stile at the end negotiate an overgrown corner to resume on a hedgeside. *At a heady 375ft/115m this is the high point of the walk!* This leads all the way on past the wood at Warrener's Bottom to swing round at the end to a gate onto a back road, Moor Lane. Turn right to commence a gentle descent. *Again enjoy massive views east to those eternal escarpments of the North York Moors.* A little past Roskill Farm, now level, take a gateway on the right just before a bend left. A hedgeside track heads away to a belt of woodland. Passing through a gate and the slender gap it runs on to join the drive to The Lawns, just to your right. Turn left on this, over a brow and down to a crossroads. Cross straight over to re-enter Snape, initially on broad grassy verges beneath an avenue of limes before a footway leads past the castle.

Snape Castle

WALK LOG

WALK	DATE	NOTES
1		
2		
3		
4		
5		
6		
7		
8		
9		
10		
11		
12		
13		
14		
15		
16		
17		
18		
19		
20		
21		
22		

USEFUL ADDRESSES

The Ramblers' Association
2nd Floor, Camelford House, 87-89 Albert Embankment, London SE1 7BR
• 020-7339 8500   www.ramblers.org.uk

Nidderdale AONB
Council Offices, King Street, Pateley Bridge HG3 5LE
• 01423-712950   www.nidderdaleaonb.org.uk

Yorkshire Dales National Park
Colvend, Hebden Road, Grassington, Skipton BD23 3LB
• 01756-752748   www.yorkshiredales.org.uk

Yorkshire Tourist Board
312 Tadcaster Road, York YO2 2HF
• 01904-707961

Yorkshire Dales Society
The Town Hall, Cheapside, Settle BD24 9EJ • 01729-825600

Tourist Information

Minster Road **Ripon** HG4 1QT • 0845-3890 178
4 Central Chambers **Leyburn** DL8 5BB • 01969-623069
1 Hall Square **Boroughbridge** YO51 9AN • 01423-323373
Royal Baths, Crescent Road **Harrogate** HG1 2RR • 01423-537300
Friary Gardens, Victoria Road **Richmond** DL10 4AJ • 01748-850252
14 High Street **Pateley Bridge** HG3 5AW • 01423-711147
National Park Centre **Aysgarth Falls** Leyburn DL8 3TH • 01969-663424

Open Access
Helpline • 0845-100 3298
www.countrysideaccess.gov.uk

Public Transport Information
Traveline • 0870 608 2608
National Rail Enquiries • 08457-484950

INDEX
walk number refers